This book is dedicated to my wife Jenny,
who inspired me to achieve what I was capable of,
my son Ian and daughter Brooke,
and my Mother and Father,
who have always believed in me.

HOW ANY TRADESMAN CAN BUILD A MILLION DOLLAR BUSINESS IN 24 MONTHS

By a Tradesman Who Has
Done It Three Times

By

Ian Marsh

EDES PUBLISHING CO.

✚

HOW ANY TRADESMAN CAN BUILD
A MILLION DOLLAR BUSINESS IN 24 MONTHS

By A Tradesman Who Has Done It Three Times

ISBN-13: 978-0-9788010-3-8
ISBN-10: 0-9788010-3-2

Made in the United States of America

Guarantee

I am so confident of my systems, that anyone who becomes a challenger and implements my systems as described will build a million dollar business within 24 months!

If you have implemented my strategies and are not entirely thrilled with the results, I will cheerfully double your money back!

-Ian Marsh

Table of Contents

INTRODUCTION

If you are a tradesman, and want to build an exciting, extremely profitable business that is fun to run, you should read this book. I wrote this book to show the average tradesman that you don't have to work 13 hours a day, and then come home and do paperwork. You don't have to give up holidays and miss spending time with your family. You can actually have a great business and a great lifestyle, something you may not have thought possible.

The life of a tradesman who owns his own business is surrounded by misconceptions. People think that you've got it made. Fellow tradesmen that work for you think that you make five times their salaries. They believe you have lots of money and they envy your personal freedom. After all, you are your own boss, you can even take a holiday anytime you want, right?

Well, that's not really the case, and anyone who's been there will tell you a story that is completely contrary to personal freedom and wealth. In fact, it is more likely to be a story of servitude and deprivation. With my story, I want to set the record straight. I want to tell what it's really like to be a tradesman running his own business.

As a tradesman who has owned my own business for eighteen years, I've experienced almost everything you can experience as a small business owner. I know what it's like to have no customers and be waiting for the phone to ring, wondering how I was going to pay the mortgage. I know what it is like to put every penny I own into my business including mortgaging and nearly losing my mother's house. I also know success and what it's like to land a fantastic contract.

But mostly, I know what it's like to work endless hours making only a regular wage for myself. I know the deep regrets of a father who can never recapture the twelve years my son spent growing up without me because I was too caught up in the business. I know the strain that lack of money and long hours can place on a husband-wife relationship.

But, I'm here to tell you that it doesn't have to be that way. You really can have a successful business as a tradesman and live the life you've always wanted and that everyone thinks you have. You can have lots of money, personal freedom, and regular working hours.

All it takes is implementing a few simple systems that I've been fortunate enough to learn and develop over the past five years.

Five years ago, I met a man who taught me some well kept secrets about marketing systems. I acted upon what he taught me and in five years, my business went from earning $100,000 per year to $10,000,000 per year just by implementing these systems. I also experienced the loss of that business. Employee's literally stole the business out from under me because I didn't have the right control systems in place. I learned a lot from that business failure and used those lessons to build a new business.

By developing and implementing the proper control systems, I experienced an amazing difference in my new business compared to my old one. Theft dropped to zero, sick days went from 80 to 5, and work quality rose dramatically. Testimonials poured in from satisfied clients and call backs decreased from around 30 percent to less than 1 percent. With these systems, I went from working fourteen to seventeen hours a day to having the business nearly run itself.

There is no mystery to these systems, they are sound business practices that successful people won't tell you, I want to share them with you because I've seen the personal devastation that owning a small tradesman's business can cause both in my life and the lives of my friends. I care about other tradesmen and I want to help you make a difference in your life as well. With the application of my systems in this book, you too, can have the tradesman's business of your dreams, and the life you've always wanted.

Ian Marsh

Chapter 1

Never Give Up!
Never Say Can't!

Since before I can remember, people have told me can't.

"You can't have that, It's too expensive," or, "You can't do that, you're not smart enough!"

With that one small word my family, my teachers and my friends all told me 'don't dream, don't aspire, don't even try'. But I have never been a 'can't' sort of person. I hate that word and don't believe in anything it implies, so if I heard 'can't', I reacted, but not in the way everyone anticipated. Instead of taking 'can't' to heart, I adopted it as a personal challenge. It became my goal to do the very thing that others told me I couldn't accomplish.

When I left home at fifteen, I had been to twelve different schools, and my grades were poor. I was told by family and friends that I couldn't be an apprentice. I didn't have the grades for it, and I wasn't smart enough.

That was all the motivation I needed. I set my mind on getting an apprenticeship and when I achieved that, I even came in at the top five percent on the exams.

Sometimes my inability to let a challenge go by took me in some unusual directions. When I was 22, my friends and I were watching a television show on the army special forces.

"You could never get into the Commando's, Ian," one of my friends told me.

"Rubbish," I told him, "of course I can get into the Commando's."

But he kept at it; "Naw, you wouldn't be able to do that!"

I decided right then to start to train. It wasn't because I had a burning desire to be in the Commandos, but I just couldn't ignore such a challenge. Before long I was a commando. The army wanted me to be super fit and super tough so I trained hard.

In the Elite Forces, there are three levels. The SAS are the top level and they are supermen. Their main role is to secrete themselves behind enemy lines, sometimes for days on end, collecting intelligence information, and hopefully get back in one piece.

Before the days of the European Union, my friend John, who was in the SAS, was dropped into Europe. With no identification and no money, he had to get back to England within 2 weeks to succeed in his mission.

This was before the fall of the Berlin wall and half of Europe was communist. It was very dangerous and he returned with exciting tales to tell. I don't have any stories that glamorous that I can repeat, but this should give you an idea of the requirements demanded by the SAS.

The part of the Elite forces in which I was engaged would take the intelligence gathered by the SAS and then act on it. We were highly trained in demolition and stealth. We would go in to enemy territory with explosives and demolish the areas that intelligence deemed high priority.

In order to do that we were taught to really ramp up our aggressiveness. It was not uncommon to go to the mess hall and see someone being grabbed by their arms and legs and thrown through a window.

A common training tactic was to have four of us shoulder a telephone pole and then go on a five kilometre march. I don't know how much those things weighed, but after five kilometres it could have been a giant redwood out of California! It would take a couple of days before we could even lift our arms. That tended to reduce the number of guys getting thrown through windows, at least for a while.

They were training us to get into areas very quickly, live off our wits and the land and have enough stamina to get home again without giving up. One of my toughest experiences was being dumped in the forest with nothing but a rat pack (that's one day's ration) and then being expected to survive for seven days while attempting to reach the "finish line" determined by my sergeant. I can tell you now that you can live on what you take with your bare hands in the forest, but you wouldn't want to!

The training that the army gave me has been a powerful ally and tool my entire life. It is the determination and willpower that I gained in the army that has kept me from giving up many times when the going got tough. I can just see my sergeant getting in my face yelling "Move your arse you scum-bucket, is that all you're made of....", (he was a bit more descriptive, but some things just shouldn't be shared). Never the less, it always works, it does actually get me off my arse and get me moving again. I have always been amazed that no matter how impossible the task, the combination of my own grit and my training in the commandos gets me to the "finish line."

When I returned to the civilian world I was proud. I had achieved what I set out to do and I had excelled at it. It may seem a rather extreme way to prove others wrong, but I had to know within myself that I could achieve anything. That I was not going to be categorized and defined by the way others saw me. I'd demonstrated this to my friends and to myself.

The next major challenge in my life came when people told me that I wouldn't be able to run my own business. As always, I set out to prove them wrong. I placed an ad in the local newspaper, threw some cable in the back of my badly smoking Ford Escort wagon, and started in business for myself.

I struggled around with the car running on only two of its four cylinders for several months. Everywhere I would go, a billowing cloud of black smoke poured out the exhaust leaving a noxious trail behind me. It produced so much smoke that the police kept pulling me over. To avoid letting my clients see the sad state of my vehicle, and perhaps lose confidence in my ability to get the job done, I would park down the street and carry my tools to the job site. If anyone asked me where my car was, I would just tell them nonchalantly that I had parked nearby.

My new business was growing, but to pay the bills, I needed to supplement my income. I drove taxis and lived off my credit card.

Just as things were coming together I decided that I needed to buy a house. When I told my friends about this, they laughed at me and said there was no way that was going to happen. Writing this I am beginning to suspect that I kept these friends more to motivate myself than for any other reason.

Money was definitely a barrier, but I felt strongly that if you truly believe in something it will become reality. As luck would have it I picked up a man from Burwood in my taxi. As we talked, it turned out that he was the bank manager of the Commonwealth Bank on Barrack St. By the time I dropped him off at his destination, he had approved my bank loan. Of course, this was back in the days when managers actually had some authority. I was thrilled to say the least.

Once I secured the loan I went to Peter, my best friend at the time, and asked,

"Hey, do you want to buy a house?" He joined up with me but even with his help, I didn't have enough to make the payments. Not to be defeated, I set about getting the money. I rented two rooms in my house to friends. I settled my brother into a caravan in the backyard, and I rented the garage to my girlfriend. I only wished my dog could have paid rent.

With that, the pressure started to ease on my finances. I started to concentrate on making my business a success. I began by asking myself;

"How do I get customers?" I wasn't doing very well on my own, so I decided to try a local company called Spinners. Spinners finds work for tradesmen. I joined up and found it helped some, but I was still not much more than a better paid employee. It wasn't enough, my philosophy has always been that if you are going to do it, give it 110 percent. I wanted my business to be a success and nothing was going to get in my way.

I was now about twenty-five years old, and as chance would have it I was about to meet my next challenge. I was sitting on my front fence with my friend who was a plumber. It was a lean time for both of us financially, and we were talking about it.

We knew if we could just make three hundred dollars a day we could live like kings. My friend was having a much tougher time of it than I was, and I felt really sorry for him. I have this weakness for lost puppy dogs and people down on their luck. Not a trait I would recommend by the way. At any rate, his wife was about to leave him and his van just blew up, so I made a brilliant decision and loaned him one of my vans.

Things must have been far worse for him than I knew because that was the last time I saw him or my van. The last I heard, he had just taken off and kept on going. I didn't call the police, he was my friend and I guess life just got too hard for him. One thing I have never ever done, no matter how hard things have got, was give up. Giving up just isn't in me. When life is difficult, that is the time to try harder, not to let it defeat you.

My friend may have given up, but for me, I decided to set my sights on making that three hundred dollars a day we had talked about.

Success is simple when you think about it. All you have to do is find someone who is successful. Find out what they do and how they act and do it yourself, and you will be a success, too. That is why it is important to have a mentor. I tried this at a job I did at the Turtle Nurseries in the western suburbs of Sydney. The nursery was a very successful company with a good reputation and they were obviously doing the right things. Surely if I could just find out what they did and do the same, I would reach my $300 per day goal. I boldly asked the owner what the secret was to his success. He pulled me close and whispered to me these exact words,

"Ian, don't worry about the cost, just get the biggest ad you can get in the Yellow Pages and watch your business skyrocket."

I was excited! This advice I felt was pure gold. Even though money was still a major issue, I determined that I was going to take his advice and worry about how to pay for it later. I made the phone call to the Yellow Pages. I assumed that the salesperson they would send would give me sound advice on what ad to place to generate the most sales.

The salesperson they sent to advise me on my ad, however, turned out to be a beautiful young lady who could have passed for a goddess in some ages. I need to say at this point, that I have nothing against beautiful women, after all, I married one. But at that moment, I would have signed anything that this particular female placed in front of me.

This is not the approach you want to take when making decisions about sound advertising practices. My first piece of marketing advice would have to be:

WARNING! Beware of beautiful sales girls!

I do honestly believe that she meant well, and my ad did pay for itself and earn me some good contacts and clients, but it could have been much better. I spent $35,000 on this ad. Yes, she was that good looking. I certainly don't regret spending this money and buying the ad, I just wish I'd done my research first. If I had known some of the secrets of advertising, that I know now, the money would have been much better spent, and while I would have still been influenced by a pretty face, I would have kept my business decisions separate from my passions.

This ad was my first major advertising and marketing effort and I began to see the scope of what could be accomplished with the right marketing methods. The Yellow Pages are a useful tool, but you must know what you are doing when you advertise there.

Between the Yellow Pages ad and the ads in the paper, I was making just enough money to keep the wheels turning on my business. However, it was not until I met my marketing mentor Mel, that I started experiencing real growth in my business and realised what I could potentially accomplish. I discovered that marketing is the key difference between having a truly great business and just a business that survives. You may be the best tradesman in the world, but that's a pretty useless distinction if you don't have any customers.

Despite the fact that many of the challenges I accepted were life changing. I truly believe that you can accomplish anything, it starts with a belief in yourself, and a willingness to take risks to prove it. The main factor that holds many people back, some far more talented than myself, is simply fear. As far as I am concerned, 'fear' and 'can't' are in the same category of words. They should both be banned, at least from your thinking.

In today's world there are so many people who have the ability and opportunity to accomplish all they can dream, and yet they never do because of fear, fear of failure, fear of embarrassment, but most of all, just plain fear. If you listen to your fears you will never succeed in anything. I have done so much in my life because I just don't listen to this voice of fear. For each person the motivation to overcome their fears and act is different. I admit, in my case the motivation to try new things has often come from a desire to prove others wrong. The end result, however, is still the same, conquer your fear and make things happen in your life.

If you have been thinking about starting a business, or trying something new, and you just can't bring yourself to do it, you need to examine why. You need to sit down and think about your reasons for not pursuing that next challenge in your life. You need to examine what is holding you back. There are many reasons why you may not try to succeed. You may be simply unwilling to try something new, which is a fear of change. You may want to try something new and then you stop and think, "How will I look to my family, my spouse and my children if I fail?" After all what kind of example is a parent who fails? This is also fear.

Maybe you are afraid of what your friends will think of you if you fail. But on the other hand, what will they think of you if you succeed? Fear of failure is a paralysing thing. You will never know what could have been if you let fears overcome you and you just don't try.

The fear can also come from outside you. Friends are usually great people, but their fear can keep you down. Starting a business or trying a new idea can be very fearful for them. Subconsciously, your friends are often afraid of change as well. You may find that when you are sitting around with your friends and you say,

"Hey, I'd like to try starting a business, I have this great idea that could be the next revolutionary idea of the century."

Friends and family often will be less than supportive because they have everything the way they want it to be, even if it isn't great. If something new comes along, things may change and many people are so afraid of the unknown, which change always represents, that they can't see beyond that.

They also may have fear that you will rise above them; that you won't be in their circle any more. They may want you to sit with them, have a drink, and just keep everything as it is.

Because of this, if you want to try something new, you can't listen to your friends. You need to remember that it is your life and your only chance to do great things. In fact, I even recommend getting away from friends who are convinced you shouldn't try. Their attitude is infectious. You need to listen to your heart and what it is telling you. Your heart will rarely steer you wrong.

Great rewards don't come without risk. If you want to try a new idea, and you've done your homework, and you really believe it has a chance to succeed, then risk it. If it really hits and is a great success, then you can move onto the next idea with a lot more resources and experience.

If it fails, you need to plan for this as well. Risks should be calculated. Usually, the worse case is that you run completely out of money and have to go get a job. You can take consolation in the fact that such notable success stories as those of Donald Trump or Colonel Sanders are littered with tales of failure. Successful people will often tell you that success is often the ability to simply endure past failure. So, succeed or fail, you will know that you had the nerve to try, and you can give it another go with more experience and a better chance at success.

Another philosophy of mine is 'don't get

comfortable.' Lots of tradesmen hit their comfort zone, and are afraid to leave it. Push your comfort zone, if you don't, you will never know what you can do!

Chapter 2

Building A Business

Most tradesmen are not business men, yet many of them start a small tradesman business. They get started in business in a very similar way. They start out training to be a tradesman. Generally to be a tradesman, you go to school, then you get an apprenticeship. You get shown technically how to do the work by your boss, but as an apprentice, you never get shown the business side of your chosen trade. Your boss usually doesn't show you any financial statistics for the business so that you would know what to expect if you went into business for yourself. He particularly doesn't want you to know what he's making. He keeps the administration of the business to himself and usually won't show you any of his marketing techniques to develop work.

He is primarily concerned with training you to be a carpenter, a plumber, an electrician, or a refrigeration mechanic, so that you can be an installer for him. This is understandable because he is investing in you and your training. He doesn't want you to go into business for yourself, it is not in his best interest. It would mean that instead of training a good employee for himself, he would be training the competition.

This is very typical of most apprentice experiences. You would expect then, that the business side would be emphasized at your technical college. Logically, you should learn marketing, bookkeeping, and administration for a small business in your trade. After all, you are already learning the technical aspect in the field. When I went through technical school, however, not one day was spent on how to run a trade business. Not one hour was spent on how to get customers, and not a minute on how to keep your clients after you had them. At the time, I didn't even realize that the business side of my education was missing.

When you finish your apprenticeship, and you're out of school, you're all excited! 'Hey, I'm a tradesman!' Then you start thinking,

'My boss pays me $20 an hour as a tradesmen, and yet, I know that tradesmen charge their clients $50-$80 an hour when they work for themselves. That sounds like a good idea, I think I'll go out and work for myself. Usually, you have friends and family that have already asked you to work for them, so you go out and start your fledgling business doing bits of work here and there. You gain some confidence as some money starts coming in. With no overhead and no expenses, you make ends meet.

The next step for most tradesmen is to

place an ad in the local paper. People see it, call you, and more bits of work come in.

Some tradesmen put an ad in the yellow pages like I did. They endure the trip from the Yellow Pages salesman, who doesn't really have their best interests at heart. They aren't selling them good advice on what to put into their ad, in most cases they don't even know. Their job is just to sell advertising space. The bigger and more expensive the ad that's bought the better. The tradesmen do see more work come in from the ad, but they aren't getting its full potential.

Unfortunately, ninety-five percent of tradesmen stop there. The Yellow Pages ads cost a lot of money and many never even get to that step. Principally, they just rely on the work from friends, the work that comes in from their ad in the paper, the work provided by a Yellow Pages ad (if they can afford it), and some referrals from clients. Hardly any of these methods do any good for generating growth and steady work for a business.

Another thing is that they are doing all the work themselves. They never have a chance to step back and see why they are in their present situation of just surviving but never getting anywhere.

In the case of a tradesman who's business starts to grow, they are faced with a new set of problems. A tradesman may think up a good ad, place it properly and start getting a lot of work from it. Work is pouring through the door but they panic.

They don't know what to do. They don't think they have the time to learn the techniques and systems that can easily control the business that they are growing. They may not even know that this is what they need. Because most types of people who go into business are hard workers, they do the only thing they know, they work. They work harder and longer. They overload themselves far beyond any reasonable limits and it becomes not only exhausting, but overwhelming.

In addition, they want to maintain control and a certain standard of work, so they do everything themselves. As they get busier, they start getting referral work and their work load increases even more. They may put on one or two staff to keep up with the work load, but they are still in the job of tradesman themselves.

Instead of saying 'This is great, look at all the work I'm getting! How do I design my business to grow and handle all these jobs?' They say 'I've got way too much work and it's killing me, I've got to stop advertising!'

As soon as they do that, they trap themselves back into their hand to mouth existence because they reduce their workload back down to what they can handle themselves. Because they don't have the proper systems in place, they can't escape from being their own employee. They are insuring that they stay within their comfort zone and stay a 'one man band'.

Most tradesmen that I know have a philosophy that further traps them in their current situation. They are working very hard, but they have a tremendous amount of guilt. They typically believe that 'If my guys are working, I should be working longer and harder than my men.' They think, 'It isn't fair for my employees to be out in the field working and making money for me if I'm out having a game of golf. That's just not right!'

Well I understand this core belief held by a lot of tradesmen, because I had it myself. We want to be fair. We don't want to take advantage of an employee. We think that our employees won't respect us if we are not working as hard or harder than they are. All these ways of thinking keep tradesmen trapped in their little box. They stay in their operations, they do huge hours and they make low to average money.

Only a very small percentage of tradesmen even realize that the decisions that they are making cause them to have that type of draining business.

Another common error that tradesmen with their own business make is they work as their own supervisor. Usually they work as a supervisor because they can't afford to hire one. Their employees are making mistakes, and they need someone to oversee their work.

They spend long hours out in field so that they don't let their hard won customers down. They make sure that their customers are being given their best service. Half the time, a tradesman is out working on Christmas day. I confess I've worked three Christmas days myself.

In addition, tradesmen don't treat their body very well. They live on hamburgers and soda, and push themselves to work long hours. Sixteen hour days are a common reality. Health wise, they don't look after themselves. They, also don't look after the reason they are working so hard... their family. For example, In my case, my son is now twelve and I had very little to do with his upbringing. I was too focused on the business and put too much effort into the company to pay attention to him as he grew. That is something I will be very sad about for the rest of my life. I don't want other tradesmen to have to go through what nearly killed me.

So that is how most tradesmen get started in business and go through a lot of their life. Many of them work flat out all the time. There is no relief from the constant pressure and it never lets up. They always have to be on call and answer the phone even in the middle of the night, so they don't let their clients down. Either that, or they don't have any work and don't know where their next dollar is coming from, but either way, many tradesmen wind up their business, just walk out, or drive off into the sunset like my friend, because it is crucifying. They go get a job somewhere else where there is no stress and no worry.

Fortunately, they can change all this, because it shouldn't be like that and I am living proof.

My story is no different. I did what everyone else did as well to get started in business. I placed an ad in the paper. I took out a yellow pages ad, and I hired a few employees.

I had managed to achieve my goal of $300 per day, and I felt I was doing okay. But my business was nearly killing me. I went along like this for twelve years turning around $100,000 per year.

Although my work was quite steady, it still was not reliable. Clients came first in every way as they were the core of the business. After all, without customers, there is no business. So, I would work when the work was available. This meant I would work nights, holidays and weekends, any time a client needed me. Personal time did not exist. My time was completely invested in the business and totally at the disposal of my clients.

Financially, I also put everything I could into the business. I invested every spare dollar back into it, only keeping enough for myself to live. It was a difficult life. The work was tough, the hours gruelling and the toll it took on me as a person was immense.

I was so completely absorbed in the day to day operations of the business, however, that I could not see how to change. We are always taught to believe if you work hard enough that you can accomplish anything. To this end, I drove myself. If I just worked harder, if I took that extra job and worked those extra hours, everything would be different. The trouble is, that the time passes by and you never do the things that actually will make a difference.

Two things, however, caused me to re-evaluate my direction, and motivated me to build my first multi-million dollar business, Marsh Air Conditioning.

The first was that after 12 years of going along the same way and not getting anywhere, I wanted to make a change. I knew there had to be a better way. I decided to start doing everything that I could to improve my knowledge about how to run a business. The first major business discovery I made was a magical thing called marketing. I met a man who told me some secrets about marketing that successful businessmen won't tell you.

Marketing is the key difference between just an average business and one that has clients racing through the door. Learning how to market your company is the first step toward making a difference in your business and your life.

The second thing that caused me to change my ways of doing things was that I met the most wonderful girl in the world and married her. My wife Jenny really inspired me and made me want to be a better man.

Since I had already begun to learn about marketing, I was very excited about it and wanted to start to apply the techniques I had learned. I was talking to some friends and I told them,

"You know, with this marketing thing, I reckon I could be the biggest air conditioning company in Sydney."

"That's a load of baloney, Ian. What chance have you got to be that size?" My friends told me. "You're just an electrician!"

Well, that was all the motivation I needed for my next big challenge. Clearly, marketing was the key, so I set about focusing on marketing. I really wanted the world to know who I was, and I put every spare cent I had into educating myself. I went to the best marketing people in the world to learn how to develop my skills as a marketer.

As I learned, I applied the techniques and my business began to grow. I started getting more and more successful. I still didn't know much more about how to handle the business. But that didn't matter, the marketing was working and my business was taking off!

People began coming to me and saying,

'look what I can do for you'. I was still learning, and I needed advice about all aspects of running a fast growing business. Plus, I wanted to achieve my goal of being one of the largest air conditioning companies in Sydney, so I started hiring consultants. I spent over $200,000 on high priced professionals that were supposed to be able to tell me what I could do to run my business. Out of seven consultants I hired, only one proved to be of any value to me.

Consultants in general are expensive. One of the main problems with paying and adopting their expensive advice is that they often don't have a clue what they are talking about when it comes to running a small tradesman business. They don't really understand the nightmares and the actual issues that tradesmen go through every day.

They may have studied business disaster scenarios in school, but most of them have never experienced the common problems that face tradesmen everyday. For example, you may show up on a job site and find that a contractor is going bankrupt and has left you stuck with $60,000 worth of materials that you have ordered for his job. They don't know what it means to have just spent all your money on materials with no idea of how you are going to pay the mortgage? Worse yet, how do you explain it to your spouse?

Or they've never experienced the feeling of betrayal from their staff stealing from them left, right, and centre. They may have read about it in their text books, and they might have their certificates, but a lot of them just haven't been in the trenches of small business.

Now, I'm not saying that all consultants are bad, in fact, there are some very good ones out there, but if you are reading this book it's likely that you are considering going into business for yourself, or you already have a business and are seeking some advice.

When you look for business advice, look for consultants who have knowledge which will benefit you and your business. I ask "What, gives you the right to talk to me? I ask them to show me their track record and their guarantee. I also request testimonials and look for a minimum of five recent testimonials. When they provide all these things, I follow up on their information.

I will go into greater detail about this later, but you should ask them about what qualifications they have to be a consultant for you and follow up on the references and testimonials that they provide. You need a consultant that had been there and can give you results, not consultants with text book answers, a library could give you those a lot cheaper.

Chapter 3

Marketing 101 – Going from $100,000 to $10 Million

When I decided to grow my business to one of the largest air conditioning businesses in Sydney, I began to apply the marketing techniques that I learned from my mentor. These techniques produced an immediate increase in my business, but more importantly, it forced me to step outside the role of tradesman and into the role of marketing manager for my business. This enabled me to see the larger picture of my business and made me begin to think more as a businessman running a tradesman's business and less like a tradesman running a business. This is a difficult transition to make for most tradesmen, and was for me also, but it was necessary.

Working as a tradesman in your own business means that you are concentrating on the work. You focus completely on what it takes to get the work done and to make the customer happy. Without this concentration, you may not only make mistakes, but you could be injured, depending upon the complexity of the installation or repair. When you are finished with that job, you direct all your attention to the next one. In addition, if you are acting as your own supervisor, your concern expands to include all of your current jobs as well as the safety and efficiency of every one of your employees.

The attention demanded by your business at this point is enormous and the responsibility is humbling.

At some point, the amount of work coming in the door and your ability to handle it reaches a balance. You can maintain the effort despite the toll it takes on you and your family, and manage to make a living. This is the point where many tradesmen stop trying to build their business, they just can't cope with any more than a certain level of work.

Many tradesmen can become comfortable with this balance. It is something they understand and to which they accustom themselves, and actually, this may be fine for some tradesmen. I know that for me, my goal was larger, I wanted to make a good living with my business and have a nice life for my family. I knew that just working hard every waking hour would not accomplish this because I'd already done that for twelve years and I wasn't progressing any closer to my goal. I was still just earning only the regular wages that I would pay an employee and sometimes not even that much.

Every tradesman in business can tell you that you pay the employees first and if there is money left over for you, that's practically the bonus plan. Your employees have the relative security of a job. You have the responsibility to make sure they continue to have a job and that they get paid for the work that they do. Not only that, but you must be sure that all the appropriate taxes are paid as well. Of course, there are also such overhead expenses as insurance, rent, utilities, equipment, and vehicle fees, which all have to be paid before you can deduct any salary for yourself.

I always have immediate respect for someone that tells me they've been a small business owner and employer for a certain number of years. This automatically tells me that they've met a payroll for that same time frame and I know the dedication and self sacrifice this means. I've watched my employees go on vacations, drive new cars and buy houses. Meanwhile, I hadn't taken a vacation for years, was driving the same car, and struggling to afford food and pay the bills. This tends to give you almost a feeling of brotherhood with a fellow small business-man that you know has experienced the same things.

Most tradesmen, however, did not go into business to work for the employees, the overhead of the business, or for the pleasure of paying taxes to the government. Most business owners will tell you they went into business for the opportunities they saw to make more money for themselves and for the personal freedom of being their own boss.

Well with their businesses owning every spare thought and minute of their time, they are far away from achieving that goal, and unless they take steps to change it, they will continue down that road indefinitely.

In order to change this situation, you first need to grow your business. You need to obtain more work to make the changes happen. You should start making an effort to see beyond your role as tradesman and start thinking more as a businessman. The main goal here is to get you working *on* your business, not *in* your business as a tradesman.

At this point, I should say that 'working on your business, not in your business' is a common business phrase that many people use. No one, however, will actually grab you by the collar and show you step by step how to remove yourself from your business and have it running like a swiss watch. I will actually show you my proven method. If you are having trouble removing yourself from your business keep reading and I will tell you how I can help at the end of the book.

The first step to removing yourself from your business, no matter how small your company may be, is for you to start thinking about marketing. You need to concentrate on marketing in order to build revenue for your company. Remember, any trained tradesman can do the installation and repair aspect of your business, but only you can build it up into the business you want.

One thing that is necessary for you to accept is that it doesn't matter what business you are in professionally. You can be a plumber, an electrician, a mechanic or any number of other service professions, what matters is not that you are an excellent tradesman, but that you know how to market your tradesman's business.

Assuming that you are still working in your business as a tradesman, you can begin small. Start by designating just one hour a week to sales and marketing. Do what it takes to commit your thoughts and efforts in this direction. In essence, you need to make an appointment with yourself to think about the different ways you can generate income and work. During this hour you are the Sales and Marketing Director of your company.

As you learn about marketing, you should begin to think about it beyond the designated time you set aside every week. Begin to focus on it whenever there is even a minute during the remainder of the week.

Okay, so what do you do as a Sales and Marketing Director? Where do you start? The first place you should investigate is how to get customers. This seems to be blatantly obvious. Of course, if you can get more customers, you will have more business, it just makes sense. After all, isn't that what you've been trying to do with your ad in the paper and the Yellow Pages? That may be the case, but we are looking at growing your business, so you need to implement ways that draw more people to you, and you need to do it in the most effective way you can, after all, marketing costs money and time, neither of which are plentiful.

At this point, I should say that I'm not going to imply that you can just market your business better and then not deliver the best service to your customers. In fact, it is just the opposite, once you attract your new clients, you need to provide them the best service with the highest integrity that you can.

Making sure that you keep your clients is part of the marketing process. You not only want to have happy clients, but you want to have happy clients that tell their friends about you, and that hopefully refuse to hire any other electrician, plumber, etc., than you. There are techniques that accomplish this very successfully and you need to implement them in your own business.

When it comes to attracting more customers, there are several factors which you should consider. The goal is not only to have more customers, but to have better customers. But who are the best customers to have and how do you get those customers?

This is largely defined by which market you want to target. If you are an experienced tradesman, you probably have some clients that you enjoy because they are easily satisfied, cause few service problems, and pay promptly. You need to evaluate the clients who are making your business a profit and then focus on obtaining more of that type of client. Perhaps in your case it is the ones with the big houses and even bigger bank accounts, or perhaps it is the working class neighbourhood that generates the most revenue for your business. Either way, you need to determine what client profile generates the real profits for your business and then focus on that group.

You are probably also familiar with the other type of client that is never satisfied given the exact same level of service. I have a friend that was called out every day for a week in the dead of winter to fix a "faulty" heating unit. Every day his client, an angry, scolding, elderly woman would meet him at her doorstep and tell him that her brand new heating unit that he had installed was broken, that it was too hot. He would very patiently go into her home, turn down her thermostat from the highest setting, which she had selected, and then cheerfully help her close all the windows and doors that she had opened because her parakeet was too hot.

These types of clients, though they may be entertaining and provide you good stories for the pub, are expensive. They require more effort than necessary on your part to not only address their needs and concerns, but to obtain payment from them. These factors affect your bottom line in ways that are difficult to measure. It is actually possible to design your marketing efforts to attract the better clients.

One of the marketing secrets I would like to share with you is: **get people to call you.** Again, marketing principles may seem remarkably obvious, but if you have never looked at it from this perspective, there is no such thing as remarkably obvious. How many times have you looked for your sunglasses only to find that you are wearing them? Obvious is in the mind of the beholder. Getting people to call you is the best way to obtain leads.

The expensive alternative to getting people to call you, is having to go find clients by mass mailings, cold calls or other non-targeted methods. There is a big difference between the kind of advertising that gets your name in front of people which is called "image advertising" and advertising that actually makes people call you. One of the big differences is cost.

Image type advertising is usually very expensive. Flashy brochures and image advertisements cost money that you not only may not want to invest but should not invest. Because of the money involved, there are many so-called advertising professionals and sales representatives that are quite willing to help you buy these types of ads in their publications.

Be aware, however, that they don't nec-essarily have your best interests at heart. Their interests lie with their job and instead of seeing a person sitting in your chair, they most likely see you as a fat bonus check. While they may know the ins and outs of layout and publication, they may know even less than you do about marketing to your target audience.

On the other hand, effective advertising doesn't have to be expensive. It just needs to work. Making the phone ring consistently can involve a technique as simple and inex-pensive as the correct ad placed in a clas-sified newspaper. The right ad can target better clientele, and motivate people to pick up the phone and call you.   To get you start-ed thinking about this let me tell you some effective ways of doing this.

Let's start by looking at a straight for-ward step by step method which produces ef-fective advertising. Each of the steps builds on the previous one and they all must work to be effective.

Step One - First and foremost, you need to get the attention of your audience. This is critical! People's attention is precious because there are only so many hours in the day, and there is so much to see and do. The way you get people's valuable attention is with the right ad headline. You need to become a good copywriter to write an ad that

will get you results. You can also hire someone to write killer ads, but make certain they
guarantee results. People buy on emotion,
not facts, so make your headline as emotional as you can. For example: Is Water Flooding Your House Right Now? Do you Need A
Plumber There Within The Hour?

Step Two - Gain interest by understanding your audience. You must get inside your
customers head. What is your customer's
problem, and how bad is it? You must ag-
gravate that problem. This means that you
need to describe the problem in terms that
make the problem real. Is your toilet over-
flowing? Do you have a horrible torrent of
smelly stuff floating down your beautiful
hallway, and ruining your beautiful plush
carpet? Does the smell make you gag?

Step Three - Solve the problem. Tell
them you can help them if they contact you,
and also how to contact you. "I am waiting
by the phone right now to solve your problem
and can get there within the hour, guaranteed. Please call 1-800..." You need to do this
in a compelling way that imparts confidence
to the audience and tells them why you are
the right person to fix their problem.

Step Four - You must test and measure.
Measure the result of each ad and if it is not
producing results, try another one, or a different headline. Start with an inexpensive
ad and keep trying different approaches until
you get one that hits and produces results.

TRADESMAN'S MILLION DOLLAR BUSINESS

Writing ad copy can be a trial and error process. You need to start with an idea and find an inexpensive way to implement it. A good place to find ideas is at a magazine rack where they focus on gaining your attention with the fewest words possible. If you see something that engages your attention try to emulate it and convert it over to your trade.

Let me give you a specific example of how to use the step by step process. The following is an ad that is "okay." It has all the right elements, but only gets "okay" results.

RICHMOND
PLUMBING

Need it Fixed Today?

123 456

EMERGENCY PLUMBING
24hr / 7 Day ALL AREAS

Domestic, Commercial, Industrial

30 Vehicles Servicing Sydney

Visit us at
www.richmondxxplumbing.com.au
www.waterxxspecialists.com.au

Using the step by step process I outlined, let's try changing this "okay" ad to a more powerful ad that will get people to call you.

Step 1: Create an Emotional Headline to Grab Their Attention.

Try "Is your drain blocked? Do you have an emergency that needs to be fixed now?"

Step 2: Aggravate the Problem

You can do this with text, or try doing this visually with a picture or cartoon graphic.

Step 3: Solve the Problem

People hate making decisions. What if they choose a bad tradesman? What if he overcharges? Worse yet, what if he doesn't show up at all? What will their husband or wife say if they choose poorly? These are all thoughts that run through peoples' minds when purchasing something so you have to remove those fears. Your solution should therefore, include some sort of guarantee, and risk reversal.

Try this: "I will be there in 90 minutes guaranteed, or I will pay you $50.00. All our staff have a security license so you know..."
Let them know the call is free such as:

"Free call 1 800..."

Providing the 800 number so that the potential client knows the call is free, plus giving a shorter more descriptive url are additional techniques which increase the effectiveness of your ad. Now, let's put this all together into an ad designed to get results:

Another point to think about is attracting attention to your advertisement by trying different ways of presenting your ad. Ads that don't look like ads, but that look like something else you want to read, like a news article can get results. People want to read news and they are accustomed to finding this format interesting. They will often read this type of ad without knowing it is an ad. Clever ways such as this can generate up to 200% more response than conventional ads. The following is an example of this format:

"THE STORY MY PLUMBER GUY ASKED ME NOT TO WRITE!"

I hope this never happens to YOU. I was getting BACK from out of town. I was excited because I was throwing a big party this weekend.

Two days before the party, when I got home from the airport, my toilet was still not working! I couldn't believe it. I had been gone and expected the plumber to fix it before I got home. It wasn't.

I was dead come Saturday! I was so irate. I called him up, yelled at my guy, threatened him , it didn't matter. He needed a part and wouldn't have it until Monday (actually he could get it but he doesn't work weekends).

I started calling every contractor in the book. I was getting nowhere. So I went to a friend and he referred me to his plumber. This guy listened, understood, and was willing to work through the night to make sure I had everything I needed.

I owe them my social status. They aren't like any other contractors in town.

Call them toll free at 1800...... and ask for their FREE booklet, "The 7 Biggest Mistakes People Make When Choosing A Plumber and How to Avoid Them." Also, ask for information about their FREE Water Audit and Plumbing Inspection which saves you money and saves your health.

Sometimes when you start designing an ad, changing a single word or two can affect the response you get, so if you think you have a good approach, keep trying different wordings. Remember, try to stand out from all the other professionals in your field. As time consuming as it may be, you have to do as much research as you can to get an effective ad. When you do hit upon one that produces results, then you can invest more money having it displayed in more places. Until then, stay small and do controlled testing until you find one that works.

Now this is an extreme crash course, but it should give you a good start to writing an effective ad. Because good ads are so critical, and doing it right takes a lot of testing and a lot of time, many tradesmen hire consultants to help them with this part of their marketing. This can work out great if you hire the right consultant, but be careful.

This book is especially designed to be a guide and help prevent your wasting money. It will also help you weed out the consultants that will steer you wrong. To achieve great marketing in your business is simple, but the subject is too large and the issues too specific to each trade type to cover here. But the goal of correct marketing is for you to develop an automatic system that will have clients flooding through your door.

If you would like to learn how to create

amazing marketing campaigns that give guaranteed results then there is more detailed information on how you can do this at the end of the book.

When you finally get an ad that actually motivates potential clients to call, you need to convert this caller into a client. This is the holy grail of advertising, but there are good and bad ways to do this. Despite your best efforts and doing everything up to this point correctly, you can still fail if you haven't created the proper techniques needed to convert a potential client into a real client.

This process of conversion needs to have the infrastructure in place so that the phone is answered promptly and properly. You need a knowledgeable person to answer the phone. Remember, you only get one chance to make a first impression. The person should be friendly and concerned but never pushy. People want to buy from some one in whom they have confidence and perceive is a friend. The way you generate that confidence is extremely important. The people you have answering the phone should meet all these criteria. In the end people are much more likely to buy from their friends.

When you've got the right ad, have motivated the potential client to call and you have the right people answering the phone and reinforcing the image of your company, you need to be prepared for an increase in business. Doing all the steps up to this point, and failing to be responsive because you are not prepared still results in lost sales. You may have customers that are calling you in droves, but if they call and your telephone line is always busy, or their call goes to an answering machine and no one returns the call, or the person who answers is not knowledgeable, they may give up. All the marketing in the world doesn't compensate for failure in this area.

You hopefully will have to hire new staff to meet the demand. With new staff on board, you now have some options depending upon your long term goals.

If you want to stay working on the tools and do most of the work yourself then I advise not to exceed four employees.

When you have a work force of less than three qualified employees, it will still be necessary for you to work in your business as a tradesman. When you get past four employees, however, it becomes virtually impossible to personally supervise the staff and keep your eye on what is happening in your business. This opens the window of opportunity for the employees to take advantage of your time restrictions. They will steal materials, misappropriate their time, and cause you huge losses, not only in labour and materials, but in reduced productivity. The worse thing is, you may not even know it until it gets beyond your ability to recover.

When you have built yourself up to this

level, however, and are serious about building a large business, then your goal should now be to completely remove yourself from the day to day tradesman tasks of your business.

Remember, when you reach the critical mass of four employees, working in your business as a tradesman is not recommended. You need to completely convert over to Sales and Marketing. You should not consider yourself as a tradesman anymore, but as the Sales and Marketing Director of your business. Any time you spend working on clients and jobs, is time you take away from making your company successful.

Despite this knowledge, however, "getting off the tools" may be difficult. It may give you a feeling of losing control. But remember, if you truly want to grow your business larger than four employees, and you have the best interest of your employees, your family, your business and yourself at heart, you will get off the tools and start managing and running your business.

There are proper ways of maintaining control without physically looking over the shoulder of every member of your staff. These control systems should be implemented as you convert over entirely to sales and marketing. These will be discussed later, and when put into place will make your business 'run itself' without your constant attention and supervision.

Chapter 4

The Worst Boss Ever

For part of my life I worked for the worst boss on the face of the planet. Anyone I've ever told couldn't believe me. My job was brutal. My boss made me show up first, leave last, and clean the toilets. I had to give up my weekends to do the company books and anytime someone did a sloppy job, my pay was docked and I was the one who had to apologize,

I was never allowed to take lunch, went eight years without a holiday and my boss made me cancel a family trip so I could take care of an emergency one Christmas Day. But worst of all, I was my own boss.

Once I heard that when you have your own business, if your company isn't a success, you aren't running a business, you're just working for minimum wage. The books will tell you that you are either running a successful business... or you're out of business. There's no in-between. Well, I have news for them, there is an in-between. The position half way between failure and success is where most tradesmen run their business, and the devil himself will tell you, it's sheer hell.

As my own boss, like many other small business owners, I lived in this in-between state for twelve years. I had created this hell for myself simply because of foolish misconceptions. These misconceptions started with my work ethic, which led to constant guilt where my employees were concerned. I believed that my staff wouldn't respect me if I didn't work longer or harder than all of them. Well, it's a highly demanding job working harder and longer than your employees.

The Christmas Day where I missed my holiday with my family was typical. But, it was my business and the client with the emergency was one of my biggest customers. Their mains had failed so instead of going on a Christmas holiday for which my family was all packed, I spent the whole day in forty degree weather digging trenches and rerunning a main circuit. I successfully solved his problems instead of my own.

I did all of the dirtiest and most difficult jobs that no one else wanted to do. I believed that if I wasn't willing to do it, how could I send someone else? If there was a difficult customer to deal with, it was my responsibility to deal with them. If there was an emergency call on the weekend or on a holiday, I took care of it. I monitored the phones after hours and was on call 24 hours a day. I would get woken up in the middle of the night in many cases and have to go out in all sorts of weather to take care of my customers.

When I started in business I had imagined that I would be able to go on vacation anytime I wanted. If I even thought about taking some time off, however, some crisis would come up and any plans I had were cancelled. I would have complained to my friends, about the exhausting hours I kept, but I didn't have much of a chance to socialize, except for business. Any way, they would just have told me "I told you so." After all, they had warned me about this before I ever went into business for myself.

One sad casualty of my obsession with my work was my close friendship with Dallas. He had been my best friend and one of my mentors since I was 20 years old. When I bought my first home all those years ago, he had pitched in and rented one of the rooms of my house. His friendship and encouragement had been instrumental in motivating and helping me get into the commandoes. Whenever I was in trouble financially, he never hesitated to assist me.

Beyond being a friend, his mind is one of the sharpest I have ever known. Any mathematical angle that existed he could work out like magic. He has gone on to be an extremely successful property developer and business person. Another thing about Dallas is that he is the most black and white person I have ever known. There is no grey area with him. Dallas believes that your friends and associates are a great influence in your life. They can affect you in many positive ways, or can drag you down some dark paths, often unintentionally.

Dallas continually advised me to get some balance in my life before I killed myself. He kept recommending that I strike a balance of family, friends, health and community, in addition to work and business.

My work commitments, however, were more important than anything else at the time. Not only did I not take Dallas's advice to heart, but I abused our friendship. We would agree to get together, then I would cancel at the last minute, or just not show up, when work conflicted with our plans.

I decided to choose work over time with my friend one too many times, and Dallas made a choice as well. He decided not to let my bad habits and unbalanced life infect him any longer. He cut me out of his circle of influence, and as a result, we rarely talk or get together these days and have only minimal contact.

This was the last and most important lesson that Dallas would teach me and it came at an expensive price. Don't allow yourself to listen to the wrong people, or be influenced by the wrong people. Their bad habits will affect you negatively until you find that you are doing the same negative things.

Your time is valuable. How you spend it and with whom you spend it defines your life to a large extent.

If you discover that someone has a negative influence on you, disassociate yourself from that person. I have had to do this with a number of people. When I found that they were not supportive and my association with them didn't have a positive effect on me, I would no longer socialise with them . This does not mean I don't help them, but I am very careful with my interaction with them.

Unfortunately, this realisation came too late to repair my friendship with Dallas, but, he was right.

Working for myself was killing me. I didn't eat well, I didn't exercise. I neglected my family to the point that my relationships suffered. I began to regret the lack of time I had for my children and missed the special moments in their lives. I know my wife felt neglected, but she didn't complain. I sacrificed so many special moments and let them slip away forever. I nearly ruined my health, my finances and my personal life. If I had ever treated a dog like I treated myself, I would have been reported for cruelty to animals and thrown in jail, and I did all this for the sake of the business.

There were a couple of thoughts that sustained me though all the years of living such a punishing lifestyle. One was the prospect that someday soon, I would be making lots

of money and the years of work and deprivation would be worth it. Another was that to
quit would mean that I'd sacrificed all those
years of my life and the lives of my family for
no reward. If I just kept at it a little longer
and worked a little harder something would
break for me. I hoped it wouldn't be me.

I'd like to tell you a true story about another tradesman that I know. His name is
Charlie and he is one of my best friends. He
has a business in the service industry quite
similar to mine and about the same size. His
business is called Ultra Lift and he does a
fantastic job of installing garage doors. Like
me, he is very committed to his customers
and doesn't want to let them down.

One day when Charlie was working, he
hurt his back. He was pulling on something
heavy, pushed himself too hard, and slipped
a disc. He went to see his brother who is a
chiropractor. His brother told him; "Charlie,
you can't go to work, you have to lie flat on
your back and you have to be really careful.
If you don't rest and put your body back in
order you will become a cripple!"

Now anyone who has hurt their back even
a little can tell you that back pain can be
agonizing. In the case of a slipped disc, you
can't move without causing yourself tremendous pain.

Here is a man in extreme pain, who's
risking becoming a cripple if he goes to work.

He's been told by an expert that he can't do anything for two weeks or the damage to his back will be permanent. So what does he do? Do you think that Charlie took his brother's advice and went to bed? No, despite the pain, he literally crawled out of his house and into his car and forced himself to go to work. With his injury, however, he could only move his toes, so he could barely drive. He touched the accelerator with his toes and drove to work at 20 kilometres an hour. Once there, he staggered out of his car and tried to keep the wheels turning in his business. He did this all the while risking his health because he didn't have the ability to let his business run on its own and he didn't want to let his clients down.

You may be hoping that there is a happy ending to Charlie's story, but there isn't. His back will never be the same now, and he crippled his health all in the name of looking after his clients. Charlie let me use his name and tell his story because he knows he's not the only one that would do something like this. There are so many tradesmen out there just like Charlie that have this same commitment to their clients and are willing to literally ruin their health, their lives and their personal happiness in the interest of their clients and their business.

Interestingly, creating this half or mediocre success, without the proper systems in place, will force you into this extreme self abuse.

People who build businesses, including myself, have many common personality traits. We are usually self-starters, goal driven and highly motivated. We also usually share similar thoughts and desires when it comes to running our businesses. Obstacles in our paths are challenges to get around not barriers that stop us. We are the kind that won't take 'no' or 'can't' for an answer. We possess the willingness to work very hard and the equal ability to deal with uncertainty. Our high degree of self discipline is exceeded only by our willingness to take risks.

We tend to be extremely demanding of ourselves and require an equal effort from others. We are also completely committed to our business ventures. Because of these shared personality traits, we truly put our heart and soul into our business. We believe in what we are doing and work the excessively long hours to prove it.

Tradesmen, who have their own business, for the most part fit the textbook profile of successful entrepreneurs. We are people who are likely to persevere in business and often can survive enough failures to eventually succeed. We have the personality type and thus the desire, but there are more factors involved than just the right personality and the desire to endure despite the hardship.

These factors are fully covered in the basic business classes, but as we've seen, our education as tradesmen conveniently didn't include these lessons. Even the most novice business student knows that you need to have several things to get started in business. Not only do you need the right personality, you need start up capital, a good idea or professional service to sell, complete support from your family, and actual knowledge of how to run a business. Most of us, however, don't consider these things when we first start working for ourselves.

Because we have the driving personality type so necessary to be a successful businessman, we don't know that we are missing a huge chunk of knowledge, we just go get started. Our very enthusiasm sweeps us away. After all, we have our skills to offer a customer, we have the confidence in ourselves and in our abilities, we have the desire, what else could we need? Well, unfortunately, most of us find out what else we need the hard way.

Basic business courses recommend that you start your business with enough capital to survive for six months. Operating capital includes money not only to open the door of your business, but includes expenses for salaries, wages, rent, insurance, materials, utilities, and advertising. Most of us have enough capital to go for about a week, maybe a week and a half. Okay, I know this is an exaggeration, but not by much.

For most of us, we don't have the option

of being well financed when we start. If we waited to be well financed, we would never get started, so we just start. We usually don't have collateral for a loan, we may or may not have a credit card, but my point is, most of us aren't really thinking about money when we get started. We are thinking about an easy lifestyle, and being able to go fishing whenever we want because we will be our own boss.

But, unless we've inherited a fortune, our resources disappear rapidly. Everyone wants to know how to make a small fortune working for yourself, well the simple answer is; start with a large fortune. We go through our personal savings, any investments we may have accumulated from a real job, and often loans from family and friends. Our credit cards quickly become charged to the limit, and then we get into the really valuable stuff. We re-finance our house.

I want to stop right here for anyone who has not put their house up as collateral for a loan for their business.... DO NOT DO IT. For those of you who have, you know what I mean, and you probably have the same philosophy. For those who haven't, for heaven's sake don't use your primary residence as collateral for a business loan. Plus, whatever you do, don't mortgage your mother's house. I will tell you more about this later, but trust me on this one, having the roof over your mother's head completely at risk, with that risk entirely in your hands is devastatingly stressful.

Even though most of us start our business with a minimum of capital, we think it is only a matter of time before our business starts to really make a profit for us. But most of the time, we never get out of the start up stage. In a start up situation, you don't expect to be salaried, or to be able to take a vacation, or to be able to build up any savings. But this start up period should only last months not years. Most tradesmen I know, and as I've told you, I am guilty of this type of behaviour myself, remain in this 'start-up' position for the duration of their business life.

A good idea or a service to sell is another important factor in starting a business. As qualified tradesmen, this is usually not a problem, and most of us provide an excellent service. We take good care of our customers and stand behind our work.

Another important resource that you must have when you start a business is support from family, friends and loved ones. We've all seen the devastating results when support at home falters, so this is vitally important. Many times much of your financial support comes from this source, but the most important support is moral support and encouragement. It is far from a coincidence that a large percentage of successful small business owners are married.

Even though we like to think that we are 'striking off on our own', or 'doing our own thing', the support of others in our lives is crucial. With someone important in our lives, such as a spouse, to lend a willing ear to our problems and provide advice and encouragement, we have a greater chance at success.

These exceptionally supportive spouses will usually not only provide moral support, but will also play a large role in the day to day operations of the business. They may take an outside job to supplement income and help make ends meet while waiting for the business to begin to turn a profit. They often will work for free so that you save the salary of an additional employee. Even if they just keep the home front a pleasant place, this sort of support is invaluable. I was fortunate to have such a spouse, and I know that I would not have had my successes without her unfailing support.

When considering what other factors you need to turn your business into a success, other business people are also a valuable resource. They don't have to be in the same line of work, the principles of business extend beyond professional boundaries. Take the time to just talk to other business people. You can share knowledge, or find advice from a number of other small business owners locally, or even on the internet. Once you realize that business acumen is what you need to help grow your venture to a profitable level, seeking counsel from others who have been there can save you years of trial and error.

If you already have a business, or are just thinking about starting one, talking to other people who have "been there and done that" can help you avoid a number of common problems and mistakes and can get you up to speed on business basics quickly. You may even make valuable friends and contacts that can help you in many other ways.

Now, since most of us have demonstrated that we have the right personality, have managed to survive financially, have the professional service to sell, and the support at home, all we need to do now is get the business knowledge. After what most of us have been through, that should be easy!

Remember, a life of self imposed servitude to your business is not the way it should be forever. That isn't what business is all about. The opportunities that you dreamed about when you went into business for yourself are still there, and within reach.

Chapter 5

The Lord Giveth, and the Staff Taketh Away

I know beyond a shadow of a doubt that you can achieve anything you truly believe in. I have proven this again and again in my life, or should I say, with my life. I don't just imagine I can do a thing, I believe with all my heart that I can do it and then focus all my energies on accomplishing it. I know I am not that much different from anyone else.

I don't have any remarkable skills that give me the ability to accomplish great things, I just don't give up. I keep persisting past the 'no's' and the "can't's" and any other obstacle that comes into my path. If anything, this one single factor has enabled me to achieve what I've accomplished. I'm just an everyday guy who's a hard worker.

But the one thing that does set me apart is that when I set my mind on something, I focus everything in my life on that goal. I essentially burn the bridges behind me and don't look back. My only option is to go forward and to succeed.

When I first boasted to my friend that with the proper marketing, I could be the largest air conditioning business in Sydney,

I truly believed that I could accomplish this. The amazing thing about identifying a goal and getting it first and foremost in your mind is that it is overpowering. I had the desire to own the biggest air conditioning company in Sydney and the commitment settled inside me. My mind was set, my path was clear!

Anything and everything I did from that point forward was dedicated toward that goal. I did not consider failure, I didn't think of being cautious, I thought only of what my business would be like when I achieved my goal. Everyday, I imagined myself in this position. I could see my company as this massive venture. I would have teams responding to the flood of calls that came in daily. My trucks and equipment would be seen at all the large construction sites with my staff installing the air conditioning systems. Everyone would know my name and how to reach me. When they thought of heating and cooling their homes and businesses, they would think first of Marsh Air Conditioning. I so completely believed this could happen, that I never looked back and I never looked down.

After all, my life of the previous twelve years was not something to reflect back on with longing. With marketing, I'd been given the key to success, and I was going to charge forward and make it happen. After so many years of teetering on the edge of failure, my vision of success was empowering!

Each day I implemented the marketing

systems I learned, and amazingly, the phone began to ring. My business exploded and my problems changed from how to get enough work and survive to how to meet the demand of the ringing phones. Many days I would go to work and be faced with too many jobs and not enough staff to send out to service our growing list of clients. What a problem to have, right? With this intense work load, every person on my staff was critical.

When a team member quit suddenly, or was ill and didn't show up for work, this meant clients would not be serviced, I would be letting someone down that was depending upon me. I can tell you that with this situation staring me in the face, I hired a lot of tradesmen with barely an introduction.

"Can you start now?" Was the first and last interview question in many cases. I didn't care much about who that person was or what he might mean to the company. At the time, he meant that a job would get done if I hired him on the spot without fanfare and sent him off to work. I remember hiring tradesmen and then filling out all the employment paperwork later. I needed a tradesman, they needed a job, it was a good match. This whirlwind climate surrounding my business accelerated. I didn't back away from marketing, but kept pushing forward and building my business toward my goal.

As Marsh Air Conditioning grew, however, so did the problems. I had become accustomed to the problems of a much smaller business where I could be intimately involved with every detail. But as I added more and more teams, my involvement became more shallow and my control degraded. I couldn't be everywhere at once, especially with so many teams on the road. Supervision was haphazard, injury was common, and the problem that began to eat away at my success started to take hold.

With my involvement in both the marketing and business aspects of my business, I had relatively few problems with this aspect of my venture. As Marsh Air Conditioning grew, however, I decided that if I hired a business manager that he could run the business and take the pressure off me. The manager that impressed me the most was a mature man, over fifty, with an admirable track record as a manager of other large air conditioning companies. Hiring this man would mean that I could devote more time to other aspects of the business and hopefully spend more time with my family.

Things were going along great, when one of the young girls that worked in the office came to me one day visibly upset. When I asked her what was the matter, she told me that she wanted to lodge a complaint against the business manager. Apparently she thought that he was favouring the other girls over her. In answer to my puzzled question, "Why?", she proceeded to explain to me. She said that the business manager gives the other girls in the office pictures, but that he purposefully excludes her and she thought that was unfair. "Pictures?" I asked blankly. "What sort of pictures?:" "Like these." She proceeded to show me a picture of twelve naked men that were well, let's just say that all twelve were standing completely to attention. I have to say I was rather shocked. "The other girls get these pictures all the time," she complained.

"Well, not any more," I answered her emphatically. Needless to say, I discharged the business manager immediately. That was my first and hopefully last brush with sexual discrimination law.

I had another wake up call which occurred when I decided that keeping up with the accounting was becoming too much of a chore. The job I felt could be better performed by a real accountant. I interviewed around seven applicants and finally settled on a very nice woman. She had all the right credentials, and following my naive hiring method at the time, I simply selected her and she started immediately. I enjoyed my new found freedom from the books assured in the knowledge that they were in capable hands. After a few months, though, I started noticing some very strange numbers in the books. The figures were not only odd, but didn't make sense. I began to investigate this creative accounting. I started to watch the accountant to see if I could notice what was happening. What I found wasn't good.

She was turning up late for work, sometimes not coming in until lunch time, and to my astonishment, she was doing the books while completely drunk! When I discussed this with the other office staff, they were all surprised. They had all assumed that I knew what was going on and was allowing it. After all, who could miss the unmistakable stench of alcohol wafting around her like bad perfume?

Unfortunately, I could miss it, and I did. I was oblivious to the fact that she smelled like a distillery. You see, before I went into the army, I broke my nose. I haven't been able to smell very well since. As she had hidden her problem so well, her alcoholism had completely eluded me. It was somewhat of a joke in the office. Needless to say, I dismissed the woman and my numbers began to make some sense again. I must admit, she came up with some really good numbers, and I missed them, but they just couldn't be justified.

I should mention a rather interesting aspect of being an employer. Even though I let her go, I felt sorry for her. This seems to be a shared characteristic of employers. When I take on an employee, I feel a great sense of loyalty and responsibility for them. Their job and therefore, their welfare, comes before mine and my family's. I have talked to other small business owners who cannot escape this same sense of commitment. It gives you such a feeling of betrayal when an employee abuses this benevolence, I don't have the words to describe it. It makes you feel incredibly sad and disappointed. You would think that the effort and sacrifice that goes into providing jobs for people would be rewarded with at least a modicum of appreciation and gratefulness, but it doesn't. In fact, it is just the opposite. I have found that the more kindness and benevolence you bestow on a person the more likely you will be repaid with hostility and disloyalty in spades.

An example of this is a young apprentice that I took on, I will call him David. I really liked David. He showed significant potential and promise and I had great hopes for him. He was a great guy, not to mention a tough soccer player. I took him on as a third year apprentice and began grooming him to take over the management of my business.

For him, I broke my cardinal rule of never hiring relatives. One day, David came to me and asked me if I would give his brother a job. He really needed it, so I agreed almost without hesitation. Soon after, David approached me again. His cousin who barely spoke English also needed a job. I agreed again. In this instance, I must add that David's cousin was one of the best employees I had ever had. This encouraged me to relax my 'no relative rule' even further.

Next I consented to give David's girlfriend a job, then her brother, and then I lost track. I felt that my initial rule was unfounded because his relatives and his girlfriend's relatives were all good people and were performing well on the job.

I continued grooming David for management and also tried to show my appreciation for his potential and talents by having the business give him gifts as incentives. The business even provided him with a brand new car. Getting David a brand new XR6 Ute was a big event. When I authorized this car for him, I had never even considered buying a new car for myself. I even authorized him taking his girlfriend on trips and staying in fancy hotels. He was lavished with presents and bonuses and I did everything I could to let him know how important he was to the company.

This, however, worked against me. The result of this preferential treatment created a monster. The more I gave him, the more he thought he deserved, and as his ego inflated, his job performance disintegrated. Not only was he not doing his job, but a lot of hostility was developing. I finally decided that we should just shake hands and part ways. To smooth things over, and try to take care of him, I offered him a job as a contractor. My thinking was that he would have a permanent job where he'd make good money. But everything fell apart.

David left and when he did the consequences of relaxing my "no hiring relatives" policy hit full measure. Half the installation staff walked out the door with him. This staff consisted of his relatives-- his family, his girl friend's family and their family's family. The loss was staggering. Not only did I lose the person who had been my best employee, but I lost a good half of my crew. How could I replace that many people virtually overnight?

After complaining loudly using colourful words for a few minutes, I moved on and lived through it and feel I came out the wiser. I can say that I have never compromised my 'no hiring relatives' policy since. I want to assure you that even though my action of firing David had such a significant impact on my company, you should never be afraid to take action because of the consequences. You need to do what is right for you and your company no matter what the outcome.

The other major component of my air conditioning business was the installation department. I turned my attention to addressing the issues that my often hasty hiring practices had aggravated. The standard mode of operation for most of my employees had become to just take advantage of the company. I tried every thing I could imagine to get them to feel the same sense of pride in the company that I felt. To encourage this sense of pride, I provided them with the best equipment available. I bought the best vehicles for their work. My thought was that showing up on the jobsite with a van that evoked awe and envy in tradesmen less fortunate than themselves would in turn give them a sense of pride in their professionalism and in their work. My van of choice was an expensive Mercedes, and by the time I'd fitted them out for work, the cost of each could be greater than $57,000.

Well, the employees took care of the vans alright, but not the way I expected. Within a week of getting the new vans on the job, one of the vans was involved in an accident. This occurred when a nineteen year old member of my staff was on a building site and was checking out a hot girl he'd spotted. He decided he wanted a better look and so he quickly put the van in reverse. Because of his age and exuberance he forgot about the tree that was located on the building site which was rather inconveniently positioned out of his view. Assuming his view included anything more than the young girl. When he felt the van touch the tree, in a panic, he stomped on the accelerator, dragging the whole length of the passenger side of the van along the tree and totalling the brand new $57,000 Mercedes van.

When an attitude begins to infect your business that results in these types of careless accidents you can't bring enough money in the door to compensate. Accidents, injuries and just general sloppiness on the part of my employees were causing havoc to my business.

Unfortunately, along with the increased work, complaints also flowed steadily through the door. The tradesmen would frequently clomp through clean homes in dirty boots, leaving a soiled trail behind them on floors and carpets. After apologizing profusely, I would pay for carpet cleaning, or make some other reparation for each incident. But, when employees don't care, the damage they cause begins to add up. I kept apologizing and paying for these unnecessary incidents. The problems were growing. There were cigarette butts left on the jobsite, trampling on groomed lawns and even minor floods caused by the work we were doing. I began to think that property damage was just an expense that went hand in hand with employees.

The main problem I had with my installation teams however was not sloppiness and unprofessional conduct. It was theft. Such nice items as copper and cable were starting to go missing. My solution was to hire a person to keep track of the materials, thinking things would become better controlled.

My choice of a storeman was a young man whom I hired using my usual infallible hiring system. If I need a person urgently for a job, the first person that applies who can speak English, is breathing, and can get me out of my predicament, I hire.

The reason I say my system is infallible is because using this system consistently gets me what I deserve, someone who is decidedly not the right person for the job.

After my new hastily hired storeman was in place, going to the warehouse became a pleasant experience. I could see the inventory going way down then building back up. I thought, this is great, we must be making lots of money However, this fantasy ended when the accounts showed there was over $100,000 worth of materials missing.

I decided to rig up a security camera to see if I could discover what was happening to the materials. The camera revealed some interesting facts. It showed the storeman amorously engaged with the receptionist. They were obviously having an affair, and of course I was the last to know. It also caught them red handed in the act of stealing materials.

Upon further investigation it was revealed that they were both way over their heads in self-inflicted disaster. The receptionist was addicted to heroin and the storeman was a chronic gambler. They were both desperate financially. They had discovered the simple answer to their financial difficulties was to sell my $1800 split systems out the back door for $300 and pocket the cash.

I turned the matter over to the police who essentially rapped them on the knuckles, but nothing more came of it. I was out $100,000 and they went scot free, but not until I'd wasted additional time in the paperwork and following up with the authorities.

But the story does not end there. During the time this storeman was in our employ I had finally bought my first new car for myself, a brand new Holden Monaro. This was back when they were first being released. Our company's carpark is located on a hill and this same storeman decided to move the industrial waste bin to the top of this hill. Needless to say, my new car was parked at the bottom and you can probably see this one coming. He went inside and didn't give it another thought until a sickening crash announced the mishap. My brand new car had a new appendage; one industrial waste bin totalling the passenger side of the car.

I decided it was time to hire another storeman. This one would not be young and full of trouble... no gambling or wild women. It would be someone more mature and settled, of good moral character and with strong family values. I found and hired a man of about 50 who seemed to fit the bill. He was an electrician and looked like he knew his way around the inventory. I relaxed and let him do his job.

I'm not sure exactly how much he managed to steal from the company before we caught him, but we discovered it quite by accident. My wife Jenny was doing a random check of the accounts from a warehouse where we purchase materials. She noticed that there was a hot water heater listed on the account.

"Ian, why are we purchasing a hot water heater? We are an air conditioning company," she asked pointedly.

"That's a very good question," I answered and we proceeded to look into it. First we tracked down who had signed for the hot water heater. It looked like our storeman's signature, but when we asked him which job it went to and how we had come to buy it, he denied any knowledge of it. He told us that someone must have forged his signature.

"Don't worry, though," he told us and assured us that he would follow it up.

My wife and I thought that it was rather odd that someone would be forging his signature, so we didn't drop the matter. A couple of days later, he came to me and told me that he had found out what had happened. His sister-in-law told him that she had gone by and picked up the hot water heater and had forged his signature. He apologized and said that it would not happen again.

After experiencing such dramatic losses due to theft, we weren't to be placated so easily. I decided to check his story. I went to the warehouse where the hot water heater had been purchased, and tracked down the guy that had handed over the hot water heater. He told me that he remembered the item and that it had been a man, not a woman who had picked up the tank.

He also said that the man looked a lot like our storeman and that he had signed for the unit and had picked it up in a vehicle with our company name on it.

I was understandably annoyed and confronted my storeman. "How is it," I asked, "that a man looking very much like you, with a signature very much like yours, and driving a vehicle very much like our company vehicle picked up the hot water heater?" I have to say his answer was most unsatisfactory and I let him go on the spot. I didn't worry about the police this time. Every time I have had dealings with the legal system, the result is that I'd just wish I hadn't.

While these noteworthy incidents with employees are reasonably entertaining stories to tell, the reality is that they resulted in massive losses to the company. Because the employees didn't have any personal concept that losing this money affects them just as it affects me, they didn't care.

I have one more example where this lack of personal responsibility hurt our company. I had an opportunity to send two of my best installers up to Newcastle on a job. Although they were in their twenties and thus still young, they were good employees and hard workers. I thought they would really enjoy the chance to spend a night in a hotel and look around the town.

Well, that evening, they chose a local pub to have dinner and began to drink. There were some pretty girls in the place and they set their sights on one of the girls. Unfortunately, the girl was also the object of another man's affection. The fracas that ensued resulted in the other guy getting thrown out of a large glass window in the front of the pub. My employees were wearing their company tee shirts and they threw the man out the window in full view of the security cameras. They then waltzed out and got into their van which, because I am such a good marketer, was clearly signed with our air conditioning company name, and drove away obviously driving under the influence of alcohol.

The next morning, I received a call from the police. They informed me that two employees that belonged to me, after all, I had my name on them, had been locked up for disturbing the peace. I was given the opportunity by the police to claim them after paying the pub owner $7,000 for damages.

I hated to let them go, but I didn't have any choice. Such reckless behaviour couldn't be ignored or condoned. The only good thing about the incident was that it didn't cause me any negative publicity.

In addition to these rather significant losses there was also the day to day problems. There was pilfering and theft of materials, and lack of employee responsibility and commitment to their jobs. The sloppiness and carelessness of our installers routinely resulted in our being called back to client's houses and job sites to redo badly executed work.

This lack of professionalism, when coupled with the theft, was having a serious impact on the profits of the company. I was determined to bring the theft under control and I implemented the standard methods to deter theft. I installed satellite tracking systems in the vans, so that I would know where all the vans were at any particular time. This I thought would boost accountability in the employees if they thought their actions and positions could be monitored. Nothing I tried even dented the theft and it even became worse.

Two main factors led to the downfall of my air conditioning company despite every effort I made to prevent it. The first involved my own sense of commitment to my clients. We installed 279 air conditioning units from Pioneer Air Conditioning in our client's homes. We found out later that they had an under rated motor. Pioneer was selling units that were supposed to be rated 18 kilowatts, or 6 horsepower. The units, however, were really only putting out only 12 kilowatts, or 4 horsepower.

That is seriously underrated. When I discovered this, I did two things. Because I am proud of the work my company does, I back it up by guaranteeing the temperature in people's homes, so I had to do something. I removed over 150 of the Pioneer air conditioning units that I'd installed and replaced them at my cost with Actron units. Actron is one of the finest air conditioners ever made.

The price for this was heavy. This action cost me my house and my apartment. I had to put all that into the company. Then, I jeopardized my mother's house. I took out a mortgage on her residence to enable me to keep my promise to my clients and give them a good air conditioning system.

In the meantime, I expected that there was justice in the world, so I took Pioneer Air Conditioning to court. I did this not only to punish them for misrepresenting their systems, because you just can't do that, but also to recover my expenses.

My vision of the justice system when I sued Pioneer was that you go to court, you tell your case, and if it's true then you win and if it's a lie, you lose. That would be justice. The legal system, however, doesn't quite work that way.

My attorney explained to me that the justice system has nothing to do with justice. For everyday I spent in court, it was costing me close to $3000, and the court case dragged on for two weeks. Because I had irrefutable scientific proof that the units weren't what Pioneer had claimed, I thought that my winning the case was a forgone conclusion. The costs finally became so horrendous that Pioneer Air Conditioning closed their doors to protect themselves and I could not continue with the case.

Irritatingly enough, although the initial company folded, they resurrected it under a different name, where of course, I could not claim any reimbursement for my losses of over $940,000.

This episode substantially weakened my company, and I was left to find some way to make up the losses. In addition I had to face the mortgage on my mother's house. All this taken together would be a challenge, but I had faced challenges before and had conquered them. What I didn't figure into the equation was the massive betrayal of my employees that had been assigned to a large housing development.

From September to December in 2005, we had a lot of work in residential construction. One large job in particular was installing air conditioning units in project homes. I had many teams on the road and each team was issued the material required to rough-in the houses. A rough-in consists of putting all the internal equipment for an air conditioning system into the house before the gypboard goes up. At this point, I was turning over a million dollars a month, which is a tremendous volume of work to track.

But, rather than do a complete rough-in, where you install the copper, the fan coil, the duct work, and the cable inside the two-story houses, they were just putting in the bare minimum. They would install a few lengths of duct to the ground floor to make it look to the supervisor of the building company that they had done the rough in. The goal of this was to deceive the building supervisors so that the work on the house would continue, and I would not be alerted to any difficulties. This had gone on for three months.

With the huge volume of work that my company was doing every month, catching the fact that the materials were missing and the rough-ins were faked in a timely matter was extremely difficult. The only reason I caught on to it was that a disgruntled wife of one of my staff reported him to me.

Apparently, this employee had a whole barn full of my materials. We went over to check it out, but when we got there, the woman's husband had loaded most the materials up with the help of some friends and had removed them. The employee's wife told us that it had taken three loads on an eight tonne truck to clear most of the materials out before we got there. We only recovered about a fourth of the gear in the barn that he did not have time to relocate.

I was frustrated and I was angry. I'd already paid for all the labour and materials which had amounted to more than a million dollars over the last three months. But what possible recourse did I have for recouping such a huge loss?

If I could get more of the materials back, that would help. I went to the Police in Blacktown to find out what options I had to punish the thieves and regain my materials.

The police were very nice, but not very optimistic. One detective honestly told me,

"Ian, you will drag these guys through the system, and even if you win, all that will happen is they will get a rap over the knuckles and maybe a good behaviour bond."

My heart sank. I knew what this loss would mean to my business. I couldn't punish the thieves formally; I couldn't get the materials back and the large housing job needed to be finished. All that was left to do was to pay for all the labour and most the materials all over again. With my air conditioning company already weakened by the court case, the cost would send me into bankruptcy.

How this vast theft and betrayal by my staff affected me is difficult to put into words. The loss of capital can be survived, but betrayal is something that affects you at an emotional level.

My staff had succeeded in ruining the company that I had invested nearly eighteen years of my life building. During that time I had employed over four hundred people. I had provided them with not only a job, but with a sense of security. I had taken pride in their achievements and had rewarded them as best I could for their work, usually going without myself. I had tried to show my appreciation for the effort that they contributed to the company. This was my repayment.

The reward for my efforts was this flagrant betrayal by the installers on the housing project. The worst part of it was that if any one of them had ever come to me and told me that they needed extra work, or extra opportunities to make money, I would have done anything in my power to help them. But this, I had difficulty understanding.

I was angry, but I wasn't as angry at the staff as I was at myself. I was ultimately responsible for this, and had allowed this to happen to me. But I was determined that it would never happen again.

I called up Gavin, the consultant that I had been working with from Your Business Angels. Gavin was the only consultant I had worked with that had ever really helped me.

"Gavin, we are in deep sh-t, buddy," I told him when he answered the phone. I summarized the problem with the housing project. On top of the losses I had suffered from the court case with Pioneer Air Conditioning, the outlook was bleak. I was on the verge of losing everything including my mother's house. I desperately needed a solution.

"If I can't have a company where the staff can't rip me of and where the company will run itself, I don't want to be in business," I told him.

This one sentence defined the creation of

my next venture. It outlined in just a few simple words Marsh Air Marketing, the company that I built in the wake of my bankrupt business. It was going to be my future.

Chapter 6

Why Get Up?
Setting Goals

At this point, the business I had spent eighteen years building was over and it was just a matter of picking up the pieces. Now it was imperative that I focus on looking toward the future. I still was not beaten and I was not about to give up. Many men, with achievements that surpassed mine, had gone through bankruptcy, in fact, most of them had failed several times. Failure is a consequence of risk.

But now I knew what I needed to do. I knew what I wanted from my business and I also knew what I didn't want. I was sure that with what I had experienced I could build a business that would not only work but be as successful as my first air conditioning company. But most importantly, I could have the lifestyle I wanted.

My ten million dollar a year business, despite the fatal flaws, had been no different than my business when it was turning $100,000 a year. I had just worked harder and had taken more risk. Having the larger volume had not changed my lifestyle. I still worked too long and too hard, I still missed important family events. I still didn't take care of myself properly or look after my health. I was successful on the outside, but my life didn't reflect it. I wanted to enjoy my business and my life. I wanted to have some time for my family and time to take vacations. I wanted to have success in the true sense of the word, which to me meant having some say in my life and in how I lived everyday.

Up until now, the breakneck speed at which I had lived my life was not what I wanted. It had always been a necessary evil in getting to my ultimate goal of a nice life for me and my family. But, I had never intended that to be my life. It had just turned out that way. If I wanted something different, I would have to do something different. I would have to craft my future for myself.

In this way, something good came out of the disastrous failure of my company. It forced me to examine my life and gave me the opportunity to make real changes. I determined that I would do things differently. I would do things right. I would design my business and thus my life and not just let life happen to me. The difference between designing your life to accomplish what you truly want, and just accepting what life drops in your lap is miles apart.

Setting goals and designing your life is like taking a trip. Most people don't just go out and get in the car and leave on a long trip to who knows where. They have a destination. They decide the best way of getting there. They plan exactly what they will need along the way. They decide whether to go straight through, or stop along the way. In addition, they usually write down, or print out directions. They try to make their trip as comfortable and enjoyable as possible. Having a great destination makes the trip even more enjoyable because you have a reward at the end of the journey.

It's not that you can't enjoy the trip to somewhere less enticing but the excitement of going somewhere you've always dreamed of is overwhelming. Hours spent in the car are made easier because of the destination. This is the same for life.

The method for getting to your destination is also important. Many cliches come to mind such as 'enjoy the journey', or 'smell the flowers along the way', but in essence, your life is the journey, so it needs to reflect what you enjoy everyday.

You may be the kind of person that wants to travel light by the straightest road possible on a fast motorcycle. You want to feel the wind on your face and the thrill of arriving quickly before zipping off to the next destination. In contrast, you may be the type that wants to take a comfortable recreational vehicle, take others with you and explore country roads along the way at a leisurely pace.

You may even want to take a trusted companion and simply hike to your destination. If your method of getting to your destination is a misery, you may quit before you ever get there.

Good directions are also critical. When you come to a fork in the road, your directions will tell you which way to go. Without proper directions, you can take the wrong road and get hopelessly lost, or invest so much time down the wrong path, that it is difficult to get back on track.

One of the most important aspects of your trip however, is why you are going. If your destination inspires you, every effort will be made to get there. If however, you are not really committed to reaching your destination because you don't really want to get there, you will use every excuse you can to take a side road and delay your trip, or even worse, derail it all together. You can see how important it is that your destination be a place you desire.

All of these elements need to be in place for designing your life. The most critical element of your life will be deciding what you really want. You need to be sure you are setting a goal that is really your true desire and not just what you *think* you want.

One of the best ways to evaluate this is by sitting down with your spouse or other loved ones and talking about what really inspires you. You need to ask yourself "Why do I get out of bed in the morning?" This question can be very revealing.

I had a friend that always thought he wanted to have a fancy house in an expensive subdivision, but when he got it, he was miserable. He had been happy in his other home in a middle class neighbourhood that wasn't fancy, but where he felt comfortable. If you talk about your goals to family and friends that know and love you, they can help you see where your heart belongs. Sometimes this clarification comes from doing the opposite of what your friends advise, but the important issue is that you have clarity in your decision. Make sure that your goals reflect your values and don't contradict each other.

Another method of determining what you want is envisioning the future and what you would like to see yourself doing everyday. You then project this out to what you want to see yourself doing in ten years. If you see yourself sitting in an executive office, running a large company, and enjoying prestige and power, that is one thing. If on the other hand you see yourself travelling the country with your spouse and hitting all the great fishing spots, you may want to design your life and your business to make it possible to sell it within a certain time frame and retire early.

You may also find by talking to your family, that their goals and desires take precedence over your own, or in fact are your goals. Your goal may just be to make your family happy and to make enough income to enable them to have the personal freedom that money provides. Your son or daughter may enjoy a sport that requires a lot of money to pursue, such as riding horses in shows. Your own pleasure may come from seeing your child's joy in owning their own horse, their own horse trailer and personally driving them to shows on the weekends. If your spouse enjoys the outdoors and camping, you can camp nearby the horse show. If she enjoys the beach, your goal could be to make sure that you take a trip to the lake or ocean frequently. These types of goals give your hard work purpose and make your efforts rewarding.

When you talk about what you really want in life, be sure you write it down. Get a journal, or a notebook and commit your goals to paper. Having goals written down is critical. In addition, the more on target these goals are, the more you will have the desire to achieve them. You can increase your focus on these goals by simply reading them to yourself first thing in the morning and last thing at night. This will inspire you to accomplish the smaller goals that you can set on a daily basis. It will also enable you to see when you are going astray and wasting effort and time. Remember, time is your most precious commodity.

When you are designing your life in this manner, there are more aspects to life and being human than just business and financial success. You need to set goals for all aspects of your life, not just making money. Not that making money isn't important, as money can certainly enable you to obtain some goals. But some things are rather unrelated, such as your family obligations and reasonable social commitments.

In my life, I enjoy family and friends and meeting new people. When I was working night and day, my social life suffered. I never saw my family and rarely had a chance to interact with friends, not to mention losing my best friend Dallas. I couldn't make or keep social commitments, I couldn't even preserve most holidays for myself and my family. My goal of growing my business to the largest in Sydney was the one overriding goal of my life and I was passionate about achieving it. But I had neglected to set goals in the other aspects of my life.

For some people, this may be okay. Some may even have revelled in all that work and the long hours as an end to itself, but it was a sacrifice for me and made my life a misery. Frankly, there are other things in my life more important than work. The work was just the means to get there. You need to consider this when you are designing your life.

In addition to the financial and career aspects of your life, you must consider such things as family and home life, your social life and friendships, your health and personal fitness, your intellectual needs and educational plans, and your moral and religious needs.

Be sure to set goals in all aspects of your life. This will ensure a more balanced lifestyle, and even though the work is just as hard, the daily rewards will offset the rigor.

When you write down your goals, make sure you do it in a positive way. Don't write what you don't want, state what you do want. For example, in my case, I would write "I want to spend more time with my family and friends". I would not write something negative such as "I don't want to miss any more important family moments." The reasoning behind this is that you are going to train your subconscious mind to task on positive things in your life. Your subconscious is a powerful tool which will work for you if you give it positive well stated objectives. You just need to believe that you can do something, define exactly what that something is, and let your mind dwell on it.

Write your goals out as completely as possible. Don't omit details as being unimportant. Every detail is important because you need to be able to "see" your goals. For example, if one of your goals is that you want a new house, don't just write "I want a new house". Be specific and describe your new house in detail. For me, I might write: "I

want a brand new two-storey, 240 square
metre home on twenty acres with a tennis
court, a pool, a guest house, and a stable for
horses." You might want something completely different, but the point is to be specific enough that you can take a virtual tour of
your house in your mind. Your desired house
should be real enough that you can ramble
around that home in your mind and be able
to sit by the pool, cook on the barbecue, and
go out to the barn and feed the horses. If you
can see it, you will have it firmly implanted
in your subconscious where your mind will
start figuring out how to make it happen.

Another vitally important point when
it comes to defining your goals is to be sure
to set your goals high enough. If you fail to
reach your goal, you will at least be closer to
your desired position. The goal should still
not be unreasonable to you, and should be
something you truly desire, so there is no
hesitation in your mind that you believe you
can achieve it. Be sure to aim as high as you
want to go. With your goals written down,
they are a guide to train your subconscious,
they are not something carved in stone.

If you realize that a goal is not as important to you as it once was because of changes
in your life and circumstances, you should
change it. Don't think of it as failing to meet
your goal but that you had the good sense to
detect that you needed to redirect your efforts in a certain way.

With your goals written down and your direction set, you need to do what you can ev- eryday to accomplish your goals. Be sure to share your goals only with people you think will be supportive. What you need are cheer- leaders, not nay-sayers. Negative attitudes from friends can influence you whether you want them to or not, and can instill thoughts that will hold you back. Remember, you are training your subconscious to work for you.

Reading your goals everyday and talking about them with your spouse, should become a daily occurrence. Look at them first thing in the morning and just before you retire. If your goals are not motivating you to get out of bed in the morning, you should revaluate them. Make them real to you and set priori- ties in your life to reach them. Incremental steps toward your goal everyday are better than huge leaps that never happen.

Evaluate your goals throughout the day as they relate to your activities. If you need to decide a direction, or make a decision for you or your family that will affect your goals, consider if it helps you accomplish them.

Actions that you can take everyday that help you achieve your goals should be taken. Those that steer you off in another direction, should be avoided. Once you have done this, achieving your goals is easy, because you will be designing your life for success. All your conscious as well as your subconscious thoughts will be directed toward making your life just the way you want it. You will be well on your way to reaching success in every aspect of your life.

My wife and I wanted our next business to not only be a success, but we wanted the lifestyle that had eluded us up until then.

We wanted to have two things. First we wanted a business where the employees couldn't steal. Second we wanted a business that would run itself. We felt if these two things were accomplished, that all our other more personal goals would fall into place. We would have the time to pursue our goals of increased time for our family and each other, and time to finally have that vacation we'd been promising ourselves for years.

I told Gavin of Your Business Angels what we wanted with the new business and we set to work making our dream business a reality.

Chapter 7

Doing It Again -
The Right Way

When you go "stone motherless broke"
like I did with my air conditioning business,
it is traumatic. I'd lost everything, the world
was at my throat, my mum's house was on
the line and almost everyone was calling me
every name under the sun.

Now, I could have just admitted defeat
and said "I'm a failure. I'm no good. I should
never have tried to be the biggest air conditioning company in Sydney." But I didn't.

Instead, I spent my genuine five minutes
venting my frustration and saying every
vulgarity that came to mind, and then I got
to work.

I knew I had the skill to build a venture
into a ten million dollar a year business, and
I had something more, I had the support and
encouragement of my wife. She was behind
me one hundred percent. I also had the
support of my suppliers, and I had Gavin, a
great consultant to help me make it happen.

Gavin was not only a great consultant, he
was an invaluable find. I'd had to go through
six other high priced consultants at a cost of
$200,000 before I found him. All the others

did was offer useless advice with no concrete steps to fix things. I will tell you how to evaluate the right consultant later, and hopefully save you the money and time that I wasted in finding a good one.

Fortunately, Gavin met all the right criteria for a great consultant. I had already sought the advice of three very high profile accounting firms to find a solution to my immediate problem. They all told me to give up, let my mother lose her house and move in with me.

Well, they didn't know me very well, or they would known that I don't give up that easily. Not only that, but I couldn't have the knowledge that I'd caused my mother to lose her house, haunting me for the rest of my life.

Gavin, on the other hand, did not make any comment for one week while he analysed my accounts, and then he said "I can fix it, but it's going to cost you." Because of Gavin's directness, his skills, the loans he arranged and his ability to roll up his sleeves and actually do hands on work in the company, we didn't lose my mother's house.

Unfortunately, because I did lose my first business, I wasn't able to own a business for three years. With Gavin's help, however, we set up a company where my wife owned the business, and I work for the company as an employee. In this way, my wife and I got a chance for a new start and began working

on the structure for the new business. We
had two basic goals in mind. The first was
for employees not to be able to steal from the
business, and the second was that the business run itself when we weren't there. With
these goals in mind, we started to develop
some control systems.

First of all we started with the employee
theft problem. My staff had taken advantage of the fact that I didn't have the right
systems in place. The real blame, however,
rested on my shoulders.

I had turned a blind eye to the theft. I
thought that I needed everyone of my staff,
no matter what trouble they caused me,
to meet the demands of my clients. My
thought at the time was that even though I
knew an installer was taking copper, if he
did a good job for the clients, I didn't want to
let him go.

I felt torn. I had to choose between the
cost of hiring and training a new installer
that would probably start stealing, too, and a
known entity that would reliably service the
clients. In addition, how would I get the jobs
done while I'm getting a new installer hired
and trained.

The cold hard fact is, and I don't think
anyone could dissuade me from believing
this after the experiences I've gone through,
is that anyone will steal if given the right
opportunity. I've employed over 400 people
since I've been in business. It has been

proven to me time after time that no matter who the person is, if you put temptation in front of someone's eyes and you don't have check systems there to insure that they won't take advantage of it, they will steal.

You may disagree with me, and I certainly wish that someone would prove me wrong, but all of the employees that I've hired over time have demonstrated to me that they will steal if given the right opportunity. Unfortunately, the way I had my business structured, it had encouraged people to steal from me.

To illustrate this, if you put a chocolate bar in front of someone for a long enough time, and they know that they won't be caught, and they love chocolate, they are going to take that chocolate bar.

Let's say you have a plumbing business, and you have tradesmen working for you. The tradesmen know that you are so overly committed to taking care of everything yourself, that you hardly ever have time to check your stock. In essence, there's no way you'll ever miss some copper or some tube or whatever other materials that are available.

Now say that a tradesman has some friends that would love to have their house remodelled, or a new bathroom added. The tradesman could do the rough in and fit it out and no one would miss the few materials that it would require.

There is $4000 in it for him if he does the

job, with no material cost. Now, this tradesman is only earning $600 a week working
for you, and the $4000 would sure come in
handy for his family. Well, most tradesmen
are not Mother Teresa, and eventually they
are going to weaken, take the materials and
do the job.

I'm sure that there may be one or two
people out there that wouldn't yield to temptation, but out of 400 employees, I've never
found one.

Our job, with Gavin's help, was to develop
systems where this temptation would be re-
sisted, and hopefully eliminated. We needed
to foster a concern for the business where
everyone would not only police themselves,
but each other.

The answer required several changes,
first of all, in the way we hired employees.
Previously, we would hire employees only
because they could do the work. As I have
said before, many times I would hire out of
desperation and not even take the time to fill
out the appropriate paperwork. This makes
for employees in the field that are relatively
unknown. You haven't found out anything
about them, and they in turn know only
what the other employees tell them about
you.

What your employees will tell the new-
comer first is that they can take anything
from you that they want because you are too
busy to check. This had the great potential

to start a new employee down the road to thievery almost immediately.

We changed that process. We developed systems and a business model that virtually eliminated every problem that we had with the old company. What resulted was a miracle. I don't use this word loosely. The systems that we developed and implemented really did make such a difference in the new business that the change was miraculous.

The difference in the attitudes of the staff and their involvement in the company resulted in a dramatic difference between the old and the new business.

My first air conditioning company was a business that was an absolute basket case. It was killing me, and the stress had brought my wife very close to a nervous breakdown. It was so stressful that the slightest little thing would almost bring her to tears.

I didn't see my son grow up. He was 12 years old and my wife had raised him almost entirely on her own. I had given so little of my time and myself because for me, my life was all business. The way I treated myself trying to run that business was criminal.

When we restructured the business and put the new systems in place, the result was a new self regulating company. The business runs itself, whether we are there or not, and the best part is, we get to spend more time with each other and our family.

Let me give you some comparisons. In

the old company, I still worked 14-16 hours a day. Because of the employee theft, I worked harder and harder and had less and less money in the bank. With the new business, I typically work 6 to 8 hour days. This alone, as you may imagine, is miracle number one!

In my old business, the staff stole from me every day of the week. The controls I put in place were easily circumvented by the employees and in the end I could not track anything. As I've told you, I had tried supervisors, storemen, and even satellite tracking, and nothing made the least bit of difference. With the new systems we developed, not one item, not one screw, not one unit, nothing was stolen from the new company.   I call this a miracle as well.

As a matter of course in the old business, employees had less than full dedication to their jobs. This was demonstrated by the fact that they logged over 80 sick days in the course of one year.   In the restructured company, there were only 5 sick days taken in over eight months. This is such a dramatic decrease, that it qualifies as a miracle!

Another major problem that cost us considerable time and money, and affected the reputation of my first company was the 30% call back rate. This meant that in three out of ten clients, we had to return to the job site and fix something that the staff had damaged. Clients would call and complain that they had water leaks in the ceiling, dirty marks on their floors, damage to the walls, or cigarette butts lying around on their property. When we put the new systems in place, the issue rate nearly became extinct. If we had one or two callbacks in 100 it was unusual.

In addition, our new systems meant that we had testimonials flying in the door and helping to build the reputation of our new business as second to none. After my experiences with my previous business, I also consider this nothing short of a miracle.

Another major problem which virtually disappeared in the new business was accidents and injuries. In the old business, I had seventy people go on workman's compensation. This is costly on many levels, including the loss of time and the handicap of having an employee out of commission. With the new systems, not only did I nearly eliminate injuries and accidents, but I also miraculously eliminated the high cost of supporting this problem.

The way I achieved these miracles was relatively simple. The systems can be implemented by any one in any size business and can produce amazing results. The secret was to give the staff the opportunity to share in the rewards of the business. In return, they individually took on much more responsibility. In fact, their responsibility increased by around 500%. Not only that, but they loved it, they were happily in control and getting rewarded handsomely for taking on the extra responsibility.

If you've been there, you know what this would mean. It was lifting the responsibility from my own shoulders and the burden distributed more evenly across many people.

When we did this, my confidence in my fellow man was restored. What I had long wanted to believe to be true, that people have a lot of unrealized potential, was proven.

This secret of giving the employees part of the business changed everything. My losses had been so great, that when we were no longer loosing money because of all the problems caused by the staff, we could afford to give it back to them as a reward. We would never have had those profits in the old company, so we were free to use them for the mutual benefit of everyone responsible for earning them in the new business.

Because the employees share in the success of the company, they would never consider stealing from it. In effect, stealing either materials or time from the company hurts the employees in a way that they understand. If they do steal, it is just as though they are taking it out of their own back pockets. As a result, they all watch out to make sure that every one pulls their weight so they don't jeopardize their shared profits of the company.

The new business model and systems we put in place were so good, that in November

2006 we sold the business for a very substantial sum. We had four companies interested in buying the new company and taking over the business. We had the privilege of selecting who we wanted to run the company rather than just having to take any offer that was made. This in itself was the final miracle.

Chapter 8

Systems 101

Business doesn't have to be tough or hard, it is purely a mechanical process based on the correct systems. If you follow the mechanical steps, you will build a million dollar business for yourself. Anyone can build a million dollar business, as long as they are shown the way and have someone there that can give them the right advice.

I don't want tradesmen letting their businesses rule their lives and stealing their most precious commodity, their time and their life. I want tradesmen to be able to build a substantial business that regulates and runs itself. This can be done with the right systems in place.

This book will not give you everything you need to implement the systems required to create a business that runs like a swiss watch. But what it will do is give you the concepts you require to start implementing processes which enable you to create the environment where your staff will feel that the company is theirs as well as yours. You must do everything to create an environment where everyone benefits, the employees and yourself.

When I succeeded in getting the staff to share the rewards of the company we had greater success with far less stress and far more enjoyment.

Because of their personal involvement, they were motivated to look after everything with the same attention to detail that they would bestow on their own affairs.

If the staff stole anything, or called in sick, they were stealing from themselves.

When is the last time you came home from work, picked up an item of value in your own home and thought, "I think I'll steal this". Well, it not only doesn't make sense, but it is rather ridiculous. That is the environment that was created for them at work. They felt personal ownership about every pen, pencil, piece of copper and wire. Why would they steal if it meant they wouldn't have as much income for themselves?

In addition, they knew they had a really good situation. Most will realize that they will never get that situation anywhere else. They have a good boss. They are making more money than they've ever dreamed possible, so to jeopardize that relationship would not be in their own best interest.

Replacing temptation with a system of ownership and rewards not only acted to increase the profitability of the company, which went through the roof, but the quality of work also skyrocketed. This was evidenced by a 300% increase in testimonials and by the extreme reduction in callbacks.

This also demonstrated how involved the staff had become in the business. You need to develop this situation in your own company. There is lots of information available that will show you how you can set up profit sharing type plans for your company. This level of detail goes beyond the scope of this book and actually would encompass an entire book in itself. In addition, implementing profit sharing is only one part of a complete set of systems you will want to put in place. With this complete set of systems your employees will develop a sense of ownership and the result will be their taking pride in the company.

From my experience, this model provides the blueprint for a dream business. Once implemented your staff will run the business for you, freeing your time so that you can enjoy life. In addition, they will most likely do a better job than you would.

This all sounds great, but what does it take to accomplish it with your own business? Once you have a plan that provides the employee an interest in the business, you need to get the right employees. This is a very important, if not crucial element to the success of your business. When it comes to hiring, you need to surround yourself with not only the best people, but the right people.

Your staff are what will make your business, and you need to build your business one employee at a time.

First of all, you need to think about your goals and how you envision your business. You then need to think about what kind of person will help you achieve that vision. Write down what you really want out of a tradesman. How do you see that person walking up to somebody's front door to represent your company to a client. What qualifications and what personal characteristics do you want to see?

Now that you have a vision of what kind of person you are seeking, you need to design a hiring process that enables you to find and employ that person. The best way to start to do this is to outline your company policies. These are documents which will put into words your vision and mission for your company and the rules governing your employee behaviour and expectations.

To determine what these rules are, just ask yourself, in the vision for your company, how do you see your employees behaving? What kinds of behaviour do you find acceptable and what kind of behaviour do you want to prohibit? In many cases, company policies are driven by the need to keep the clients happy, so, what set of guidelines do you want your employees to follow to ensure that clients and their property are treated with respect. Before hiring anyone for a position in your company, these guidelines should be written down.

Consider including the following elements in your employment policies:

Job Site Policy
Lunch/Break Policy
Job Safety Policy
Bonus Policy
Equipment Policy
Uniform Policy
Vehicle Policy
Customer Payment Policy
Mobile Telephone Policy
Absence/Late Policy

Your policies should clearly present what you will and will not tolerate in your employees. They should also include what you expect from your employees and what they can expect from you.

For example, a few things that I will not tolerate are arriving to work late. I don't tolerate staff smoking in front of clients or leaving cigarettes or butts lying around. I also don't tolerate my staff walking on customer's carpets with their shoes on.

An example of some of the things I expect of employees is for them to treat a client's home like their mother's house. No, that does not include taking out a mortgage on it to attempt to save their business, that doesn't work, as I know from personal experience. I expect them to roll drop sheets down everywhere they will be walking in a client's house, so that their shoes never touch the floor. I expect them to be tidy and clean at all times. If a job runs late and goes past their normal working hours I expect them to stay and finish the work. I also expect them to occasionally start early or work weekends. I have all these expectations written down in my employment policies.

Once you have your policies completely outlined, you need to use them properly in your selection process.

When interviewing a new person, you sit them down, and talk to them. One of the first things you should do is give them a copy of your company and employment policies and allow them to read them. This should give them a good overview of the vision you have for your company and your expectations for your employees.

When I talk to an applicant, In addition to such basic questions concerning their prior work experience, I also ask some questions designed to give me an idea of their stability and dependability. I ask them such questions as:

Do you own a vehicle?
Do you have a driver's license?
(Request to see it and photocopy it.)
How long does it take to get to work?

I also ask how they feel about my policies and expectations. I ask them questions which will reveal if they will be able to comply with my requirements, for example:

Is there any reason why you could not work past 6 or 7 p.m. Monday to Friday? Would starting at 6 a.m. occasionally pose a problem for you?

I also ask them if they have a problem talking to clients about additional items they see that the client might want to buy. I'm not really expecting them to be a salesman, but if they see the opportunity to just be honest with a client and tell them simply, "If you do this, these are the benefits you can have. We offer this service for you", they will very likely generate additional work with a client.

Being this specific with an applicant up front by explaining your policies and the consequences of not adhering to them will help that person know if a job with your company is for them or not.

Before you short list a candidate, or spend any more time and money evaluating that person, you should phone their last boss to ask for a reference. You may think their former employer won't tell you the truth but I can tell you from experience that they generally do and the biggest mistake you can make is not to call them.

When you have interviewed the potential

employee, and checked their references you should also test their skills. As part of your evaluation process, you should send them out on a job with your staff for a day (paid, of course) to assess their technical skills.

After confirming their skills, there is another test you can apply which will provide more in depth screening. Because there are some costs associated with this test, this should be done at the end of the interview process when you are reasonably sure that the person is a good candidate for your position. When you compare it to the cost of losing a staff member, the cost of the test is trivial. Losing staff is very expensive, so if you follow the correct processes in hiring, you will save a fortune.

This additional test is a personality test, and can play an important part not only in the final selection process of your employee, but in finding where they fit into your organization. Imagine your business is a bus. You are the driver of the bus, and your passengers are the staff that keep the bus going. You must have the right people sitting in the right seats on the bus. An amazing way to do this is with a personality profile. Once you have gone through the evaluation process and you are very interested in a potential employee, have them complete a personality profile questionnaire

If you get them to do this questionnaire you will be amazed at how accurate the profile is. It will let you know if someone is prone to lying to avoid getting in to trouble, or if the person is meticulous about fine detail which would tend to make them a great administrator.

The program I found and use is so powerful that I rate it as one of the most critical elements to ensure that I have found the right person to join my team.

When I select a person, I have them sign an employment contract which describes what you and the employee expect from each other. Having this contract is important in making sure that there are no misunderstandings on this account.

I consider all these things to be essential factors when employing every staff member. Unless it is a special situation, I don't just hire someone to solve a problem and make customers happy. When you do that, chances are your hasty decision will cause you many more problems later.

If you have visualized what your company should look like and how it should function, then make sure that the employees that you hire fit into your vision. Don't settle for less. Don't think that because good people can be difficult to find, that you are setting yourself up with an impossible task, because you aren't.

You need to know the type of staff that you want and stick to your ideal. They are out there and they do want to work with you.

I say work **with** you, not **for** you, because if the staff is working with you, everyone is getting a benefit out of what is happening in the company.

You just need to be determined enough to search until you find those people. When you do find them, take care of them the very best that you can and hold onto them. If you don't, and you accept any ol' person off the street, your business will soon deviate dramatically from your vision.

Perhaps, in an ideal world, you will have the option of taking your time and hiring carefully in all cases, but in the real world hiring mistakes do happen. When this occurs and a staff member doesn't tow the line, or fails to meet your expectations, you need to dismiss them.

In addition, there will be times when, out of necessity, you just have to hire someone that is not the perfect choice for your company.

For example, say that you're an electrical contractor and you have a lot of work going on. One of your staff just quit and you have clients desperate to get work done. Your first inclination is to get another tradesman quickly.

In the past, you wouldn't have spent a lot of time thinking about the tradesman that answered your ad. Especially in terms of the value that they will add to your company. You would probably just think that you need to get another tradesman quickly.

When in this situation, you don't think of the appearance of that person and the image he projects of your company. The tradesman's primary qualification is that he just happened to come in the door at an opportune time. He shows his trade license, tells you he's an electrician, so you send him out on jobs to take care of your clients. I should point out right now that we are talking about your clients, not someone else's clients.

You understand that you can't let your clients down but you don't want to sacrifice your vision of the company long term. So what can you do if you are absolutely desperate?

First of all, you need to remember that you **never solve a long term problem with a short term solution**. Your staff are the components that will make your business.

You may have put him on, but you should continue with your evaluation process. Unless he meets all of the criteria that you expect from a long term employee you should consider this as a temporary situation and you should still be advertising until you can find someone better. You should make certain that the tradesman that you've hired knows that his position is "probationary", and that you are giving him a chance to prove himself. He may rise to the occasion. If he doesn't, replace him as soon as you can.

With tradesmen and the installation aspect of your business, this system of hiring can work well. But, what about the administration staff? This is another area altogether, but it follows the same principles, only more so. With critical positions, such as accounting and management, you will also need to find the very best people.

I want to point out that I hardly had any issues with my administrative staff and I had one of the best sales teams in Australia. It was mainly the installation teams that were the issue.

When hiring for an administrative position your search should be for the most meticulous and organized person you can find. They need to look after every minute detail for you and not let anything get past them. Because this person is so crucial to the success of your business, you will want to find just the right person and make certain that they fit with your vision for the company. Remember, these positions have responsibilities for issues which can affect everyone in the company. I can not emphasize enough how important it is to collect the right people around you.

When you advertise for this person, you should put down exactly what you require in the ad. Don't be shy and think that someone with university qualifications wouldn't want a job in your office because, based on my experience, they will. Your job is to determine exactly what the qualifications should be and exactly what their job description is going to be. Keep searching until you are confident that you have found the perfect person. They should have fantastic skills in administration and if the position involves accounting they should be able to make sure your accounts are absolutely accurate.

Follow your standard hiring procedure. Do not skip any step despite the difference in job descriptions. Once again, you will sit down with the person you are considering for your administrative position, and you set out the guidelines. You need to remember that it has to be a win/win situation for both of you. You can't expect them to give you 200% effort if you are not going to give them a reasonable reward for it.

One of the major errors I made in my other business was that I didn't have that professional person there keeping an eye on everything and tracking every aspect of the business. I would have caught things sooner and could have prevented a lot of the problems we developed in my business if I had known how to hire correctly.

If you follow the steps I've outlined, you will dramatically improve your chances of getting the right staff member.

In addition, I should also mention changes we made in collecting unpaid accounts. The number of times I have been caught by clients not paying their bill is incredible. The lesson I learned was that "possession is nine-tenths of the law." It was amazing how quick someone could find the money when their air conditioner was suddenly no longer on the side of their home. After you have completed a job, a client feels less and less obligated to pay for the services rendered. Because of this we began to politely remind the client that they would need to have a cheque for the full amount on completion of their job.

If the client did not have a cheque after already being advised to have one ready, you can be justifiably suspicious.

Now if you are like me, you probably feel a bit embarrassed asking for the money, so you just tell the client that it will be alright to pay later when they can, but that can mean disaster. The bottom line is that you must institute a step by step process to collect money owed. When all reasonable efforts have been made to collect the debt, you should take back your equipment as quickly as possible. Do not let it drag on. (You should consult your lawyer, but it helped me greatly in the new business when I instigated firm payment policies.)

As part of the process of getting the right staff on board, it is critical that you look after them as best you can. When everyone is chosen carefully and understands the common goal that you are all working towards in the company, everyone will be rewarded accordingly.

Over the years I have hired over four hundred staff for my businesses. Having that experience doesn't make it any easier to fire them. For me, saying goodbye is just as hard the 400th time as it is the first time. It is not enjoyable but it is an important part of the staffing process.

Sometimes a little voice inside your head will tell you that a person you are considering hiring or firing is not right. It is like an instinct, or a sense, and honestly, the number of times I wish I'd listened to that little voice instead coming up with excuses to ignore it are too numerous to count.

Many times, if I was having trouble with an employee, I would over ride that little nagging voice and give them one more chance. Or, I'd make excuses for them and rationalize that it didn't matter if they'd turned up fifteen minutes late nearly everyday for the last week. Or I might overlook a certain behaviour thinking that a staff member might have had a really good excuse for what they did.

All the time, that little voice would be screaming away telling me not to ignore it, but to take action. The little voice was right. All those little things add up to tell you that the person is not the right person for you. It lets you know that the person could do a lot better and that this is not your vision of how the staff for the company should operate.

So when these little things happen, listen to that voice and dismiss that person immediately! Do not hesitate! Do not weaken in your resolve! Trust your sixth sense that the person is not right and work on the quickest way to remove them from your company. If you hesitate, there may likely be collateral damage, This basic principle I've outlined can be summed up with the following statement: hire slow and fire fast!

Sometimes, you can hesitate to fire someone for several reasons. Some reasons are rational and should be given consideration, and other reasons are motivated by fear and doubt. You need to identify which type of reason motivates your hesitation and deal with it. If it is a rational reason, for example, I have had staff that performed well for quite a while, and then suddenly started to show signs of trouble. In one instance, the staff member began to show up late without an adequate explanation. Another failed to do their work to their usual high standard.

If they are normally a good employee, you need to bear in mind some people have off days and every now and then you may even have off weeks where you can't perform at your peak. In this case, I have often made allowances for my top performers. I came up with methods of rewarding them on a regular basis.

One of the methods I use as part of my

organization is to schedule regular breaks for the staff. Every couple of months, I let them have an extra day or two off and give them a long weekend. You can tell them that because they are doing a fantastic job, that you want them to take two days off, for example, Friday and Monday. They can take their family somewhere they might enjoy, and you pay for it. You tell them, "Here are some tickets for you and your family, go and enjoy yourself!"

It has cost me a little bit of money but in the end, the rewards are there, because it tells your employee that you know they are trying and you appreciate them. Plus it gives them a rest that they may particularly need.

You have to be extremely careful with these types of rewards. You need to make absolutely certain that there are no alarms going off warning you that it is time to terminate an employee. For this reason, I have another principle: **never solve staff problems by throwing more money at them.**

When an employee starts giving you trouble, you need to first evaluate if they love what they do and are happy, or if they don't and are unhappy.

First of all, I am assuming that you pay them very well for what they do. Make sure you are right at the upper limits of what is doable for you. If you have a situation where an employee keeps asking for more and more or you keep trying to make them perform better by giving them more money, don't expect positive results. It is time to seriously consider your path forward with this employee.

What will more likely happen is that they will become a leach. They will actually start sucking more and more resources out of the business and delivering less and less.

This usually pushes them into the category of unsalvageable. You may want to give it one last try but do not go beyond this.

The best course of action is to meet it head on. Do not put this off! At the first sign that what you have already tried is not working, sit down with that employee and talk to them. Find out if they are dissatisfied in a way you can rectify. You should ask them to tell you what's on their mind. Are they happy or not? If not, is there anything you can do to make your business a place they love to come to? If the answer is again no, you need to say goodbye to them quickly. Thank them for their service thus far, and tell them they need to find a better career opportunity for themselves.

Don't be afraid to have that conversation because you will probably be doing yourself and the employee a big favour. If they are not enjoying what they are doing, they shouldn't be working for you. There is nothing you can do to change that. They've got to love their job to be an effective employee.

When an employee cannot be salvaged, and needs to be fired, don't hesitate to do it. You may want to hesitate out of fear, for example, you may believe that you won't find anyone better. However, if you wait, you are just setting yourself up for disaster.

You may think that if you fire a person, you will not be able to carry on with business as usual. I'm telling you now that you *will be able to* carry on, that a solution *will* come up, and you *will* survive.

If you have to let a couple of clients down, all you have to do is ring those clients up and explain. They should understand if you take the following approach. You just tell them, "I have had to let an employee go. They honestly don't meet our standards for the company and rather than damage my reputation with you, I'd much rather say goodbye to them, get them out of the company and find another person. I'm very sorry, but I will have a person out there as soon as possible."

That's what you have to do and I've found that usually they understand, especially if they are another business.

If I had known this when I had my first business, everything would have been different. I understand now that I created the situation I was in with the employees through not acting when I knew I should.

I should have taken action when I had an employee that was calling in sick every third week. I should have taken action when I knew I had employee who was stealing copper. But despite the little voice screaming at me in the back of my head, I failed to take action.

It is not a comforting thought that my ten million dollar a year business came undone because of my lack of employee management skills. However, this was certainly a specific element in the failure of that business.

Remember, you need to visualize your company the way you want it to be and hire people that fit your vision. If you have to hire less than the best out of necessity, let it be on a temporary basis and be constantly looking to get better people.

Don't hesitate to fire someone that is not meeting the standards you have set for your employees. And the most important thing of all, make your employees part of the company and reward them handsomely. If you do your business right, it will run itself and be the business of your dreams!

Chapter 9

Helping Other Tradesmen

I want you to think about something. If you could ask anyone in the world for advice about your tradesman business, who would you ask? Would you ask a fellow tradesman that was struggling along like yourself, or would you want to ask a tradesman who has made a success of his business and his life?

Imagine the largest tradesman business in your area. You know, the one with the latest equipment, new clean vans with their name displayed on the sides, and all the best jobs. You probably know the business's name as well as your own because you see it everywhere. Imagine being able to walk into the owner's office and sit down and talk to him like a friend. Not only that, but imagine that he would actually listen to your problems and even answer your questions with good relevant advice. Would you do it?

Well, I want you to know, that I am that person. I have had one of the largest air conditioning businesses in Sydney and I built it from the ground up. I have been the one with all the beautiful vans with the insignia, the best jobs and the latest equipment. I have both lost that business, built it again, and sold it for a handsome profit. I have been there and done that. I know how to succeed and just as important I know how to fail. I have sat in that office that you just imagined, and I actually want to help you and provide you with the advice you need to succeed.

First, however, I want to tell you what I believe to be the most important thing to know when you are looking for advice and guidance from a professional. This involves asking one critical question to anyone you consider as a consultant and anyone you want to hire with your hard earned money. The question is: "What gives you the right to talk to me?" You need to remember this question and use it when you seek advice.

Now, I specifically want to answer that same question for you just as though you had personally asked me; "What gives you the right to talk to me?"

I have two reasons for wanting to answer this question, first because you should ask me, and second, because I have the answer you need. I want you to know that I am the best qualified person you will ever find in this field and that I am qualified to help any tradesman, anywhere in the world. I'm qualified, because I've been there. I didn't learn my business techniques out of books. I learned them by experiencing them. I have survived almost every problem, disaster, and even success that can possibly happen to a tradesman in business. I've experienced them first hand and I've found solutions for them; some which worked, and worked well, and some that didn't. But, the main reason I would say that I have the right to talk to you, is that I understand how to build a successful business in the trade industry. I've created and run three multi-million dollar businesses and I want to help you improve your business and make your business a success.

My first business, I personally built from a struggling venture with a turn over of just $100,000 a year into a business doing ten million dollars a year, and I did this in just five years. I then lost everything because I was naive and didn't have the proper systems in place. At that point I developed the proper systems, and built a second business, Marsh Air Marketing. This became a multi-million dollar business within eight months. I then built a third business, my internet business which turns over a million dollars a year.

These experiences give me the ability and the credentials to help the average tradesman build his business into a success. Not only that, but I can help him to put into place the right systems which will enable him to have a normal life with regular hours. Isn't this what every business owner wants?

Not only can I tell you how to handle success, but I can tell you how to handle failure, because I've been there, too. When you've been at the top of a ten million dollar a year business, and then lose it, the way back down is steep and tragic. I am quite proud to have maintained my credibility in the market place despite the loss of my business. I even have testimonials from companies that I ended up owing hundreds of thousands of dollars. This is because I know how to fail as well as I know how to succeed.

Not every businessman can suffer a loss of the scope and magnitude that I did and still be able to rebuild with the confidence of his peers.

So, based on what I've accomplished with my businesses, both good and bad, I have the right, and in fact, in many ways, the requirement, to talk to any tradesman about their business and help them grow theirs into the business of their dreams.

Now, on the other hand, I don't have any right to talk to you about financial or legal advice. Even though my businesses included being knowledgeable about both finances and legal issues, I am not an attorney nor am I a licensed financial adviser. When you do seek financial or legal advice, remember, always ask for references. Talk to those references.

This goes hand in hand with asking them the question, 'What right do you have to talk to me?' Again, once you have asked this question and been satisfied with the answer then request references. Do not hesitate to check the references and get testimonials from former clients. I cannot emphasize the need for testimonials enough! The best form of reference is what a consultant has done for another client. Don't be hesitant to ask for results, and then don't fail to follow up.

If you are going to give your money to someone to help you, don't just rely on their paper credentials and the fact that they have a nice suit, or an expensive hair cut. A professional in any field will have pieces of paper like an MBA or CPA, but that is not the paper you want. You want a piece of paper that gives you the contact information of several references. If you can, you should call every person on the list. The larger the sum of money you are considering spending, the more you should investigate. In addition, evaluate any information you can find about them on the internet, or from professional organizations.

What you are looking for are clients that are extremely happy and overwhelmed with the quality of service that the person has given to them. Find out what they have done and compare it to what you need. Find out if the consultant provided the reference with the same type of service that you are considering. It will do you no good if a consultant provided advice on marketing and you need advice on financial controls.

If a consultant is reluctant to give you references, beware! People who have references and client testimonials also have another thing, they have integrity. Without integrity, you won't get testimonials from your clients. In order to get clients willing to support you with testimonials, you've got to be straight and honest. You've got to tell it like it is, not like someone wants it to be. Clients value this in a consultant and are willing to tell others about how you've helped them.

After I built my second venture into an eight million dollar a year business in just eight months, I wanted to do something else. I knew that everything I had learned and all the systems I had developed could be used by any other tradesmen to make their businesses a success. After witnessing so many struggling tradesmen for so long, and having been one myself, I decided I had to give back to the industry. With the use of my information, other tradesmen could escape a life of half success and endless work!

I knew I could make a difference and I was inspired to help. At that point my wife and I decided to sell the new business we had created, which would then permit me to devote my time to helping other tradesmen make their businesses a success.

Since then, I have helped many tradesmen massively improve their businesses and change their lives for the better. But, I don't want you to take my word for it. Remember, I told you that you should always get refer-

ences and testimonials and check them before you take anyone's advice. This includes
taking my advice as well.

The following tradesmen have given me
permission to share their testimonials with
you.

Ian Jack of Blacktown Rainwater Tanks
P/L wrote and told me: "Its only been 6
weeks since I received your information and
already I am getting three or four more jobs
a week. This is powerful stuff!"

Another tradesman, Charles Abdullah,
A.W.S P/L, of Punchbowl, wrote and said: "I
have been in business for 14 years, I didn't
really believe your claims but I thought I
would try it just out of curiosity.

Ian, this is like a miracle! I have got so
much work now I have a totally different
problem. How do I keep up? Thank you. This
was a great investment!"

Craig Richards General Manager of BBY
International P/L, in Brisbane, told me, "Ian,
I just wanted to thank you. That idea you
gave us with the recorded message is incredible. We spent $500.00 on the ad in the local
paper and we received over 50 leads from it.
I have never seen such results!"

"I went from $500.00 to $2000.00 a week
in just four weeks of using your system.
Thanks, Ian!" George Vella, Bill Bell Plumbing P/L Victoria told me.

I have helped all these tradesmen to
change the way they do business, and have

headed them toward success. I can't tell you how rewarding it is for me to help someone turn their business around and change their life! I want to help you do it, too!

In regards to testimonials, you need to remember that you are also a professional consultant to your clients. If you are honest and straightforward with them, and you have the proper controls in place so that everyone in your business treats your clients properly, you will be a success.

I have always dealt with everyone fairly and honestly, it is part of my basic nature and not something I could change even if I wanted to. When my first business failed, I didn't change the way I did things. I strongly believe that you must have integrity no matter what the situation or the cost. I went to every supplier that I owed money and talked to them. I sat down face to face with them and explained what had happened to my business and I apologized. I didn't know what else to do. As difficult as that was, I wanted to do it. When I let someone down, it really affects me.

I was surprised by the response from my suppliers. No matter how much money I owed them, and believe me, the debts were significant, they were, with only one exception, very supportive.

Of the rest, I want to relate one amazing example of the support I received. This support came from Advantage Air. I want to mention them in particular because their support was above and beyond what I could ever have imagined! When my business went bankrupt, Advantage Air was by far my largest creditor. I owed them hundreds of thousands of dollars and they had no hope of ever receiving a dime.

Instead of them taking every action possible against me, and discrediting me in the industry, they did something unexpected.

David Devoy, the general manager of Advantage Air, flew all the way over from Perth, a trip which is a minimum of four hours by air, and addressed the staff of the new company. He stood up in front of everyone, put his hand on my shoulder, and said,

"We have the utmost faith in Ian. He is one of our finest clients, and we support him 200% in any venture that he decides to put his efforts into."

I can not tell you how much this meant to me. To this day I still maintain a business relationship with Advantage Air and with the other companies that supported me. I also treasure their association. I could never put into words my heartfelt appreciation for this group of professionals and will never forget their kindness and encouragement when I truly needed it the most.

Chapter 10

Epilogue

If you are reading this book, you are very likely a tradesman who either has a tradesman's business or are considering starting one. I wanted to tell you that I wrote this book for you. Having my own tradesman's business nearly killed me, and I mean that literally. If you've been there, you know what I mean. If you haven't, then I don't want to scare you away from starting a business, but I want you to know that it doesn't have to be that way.

I struggled along like everyone else for eighteen years. It wasn't until I built the second company Marsh Air Marketing P/L that I realized that business does not have to be hard.

As a tradesman, you probably feel that you do not get the recognition you deserve in society. Most people think not only that we charge too much, but that we are unprofessional, and the most unreliable people in the world! Well I want to set the record straight.

We are the backbone of society, we have one of the most dangerous and challenging responsibilities in the world. To illustrate this, when was the last time you heard of an office worker falling to her death or getting electrocuted? But, despite being under-appreciated, we get very little reward or enjoyment out of our businesses. We work hard and face all the discomfort and danger for only a regular wage. Well, we may not be able to change the attitude of society overnight, but we can at least get rewarded monetarily for all our dedication and hard work.

Because of my experience and extensive research into what makes a successful business, I can teach you how to create a million dollar business yourself. You can accomplish this within two years if you just follow my simple step by step processes. That is only two years before you can actually have a nice life and a full bank account. I know many of you have worked far longer than that and don't have much to show for it!

I have put all of my hard earned knowledge into structuring a "get out of jail card" for any tradesman that needs it, and it is my mission to ensure that this information is there for your benefit.

So, what do you do to make your own business successful? Where do you start with limited resources. What steps do you take to make your tradesman's business grow and what do you do to make it become an enjoyable way to make a living?

This book will give you a start and help you to see the potential that is out there for your tradesmen's business. But, because of the limitations of this book, and the vast amount of information I have assembled, the book is just a first step. To really put your business on a fast track to success, you need a personal mentor that knows your industry. I can assure you that I have all the trial and error experiences necessary to help you avoid the failures and the rocks in the path. You can just implement the successful techniques I'll give you and you can have your business making the kind of money you need for the lifestyle you want and deserve.

The next few pages will give you an executive summary of the system I have developed. However, when you get my complete package you will have all the information you need to make your business a success.

I took everything I knew about marketing and in addition studied and researched the subject extensively. I spent over $150K on that research, going to high priced seminars, hiring copywriters, testing ads, sales letters, client newsletters, newspaper ads, etc. I then tried it out with a number of other contractors, and the results were amazing! The "Simple System" I created will turn any ordinary tradesman's business into a "high income, high profit machine".

I also back up what I say with a guarantee. Remember, you should always get in writing what a consultant will provide you!

My guarantee is that if you use my system for a year you will add at least $70,000 turnover to your business. That is $70,000 that you know you would not have made without using my System. If you don't add at least $70,000 to your turnover just send me proof that you used at least 10 of my strategies, ask for a refund, and you've got it .... every cent, after 12 full months! I do reserve the right to print your letter.

In addition, you also have a full 90 days to examine everything, and to test and use my strategies. If you don't get the same kind of results as the other tradesmen who have used my system, then you can simply put it all back in a box, return it, and get a full, 100% refund issued the very same day we receive the materials. No questions. No hassles. No hard feelings. You MUST be completely satisfied. If not, I want you to ask for and get a refund.

My system really works, don't forget, I've done this three times for myself and many times for others. That is why I have no hesitation giving you this iron clad guarantee.

Following are a few highlights of my system to give you an idea what it includes. With the complete system I show you how to:

- Add $1,000 a week to your income by "target marketing" to upscale homes and businesses (I'll tell you how to choose them and get their attention).

- Stop wasting money on ads that don't work or can't be held accountable.

- Stop being the "prey" of advertising reps and ad agencies.

- Use direct mail effectively.

- Double or even triple your profits from coupon-type advertising.

- "Educate" your customers, so they want you to do ALL their work and will never dream of calling anybody else.

- Get up to 40% of all your new business free, from referrals!

- Increase your profits per job, on almost every job.

- Get corporate decision-makers to choose you, seek you out – and get "cheapest bid" out of their heads!

- Implement "auto pilot marketing." even the laziest tradesman can skyrocket his business with these techniques!

- Use "inexpensive postcards" to re-activate old customers.

- Uncover "hidden profits" in your current customers.

- Develop extra "profit centres" that make sense.

- "fire" a customer – and how doing so will increase your profits!

- Find additional money hidden inside your customer list.

- Keep your current customers coming loyally back!

That's only a tiny part of my system. Yet using even just a few elements of this system can cause your income and profits to sky-rocket.

By the way, it doesn't make any difference if you have a formidable opponent right across the street. It also doesn't matter if all around you, your "friendly competitors" are piling up debt to their eyeballs just to keep going – or dropping like flies. None of that matters.

My system will reveal "hidden gold mines" right there in your city or town, even in your own business. My system will show you how to revitalise your profits. It will tell you how to attract really great new clients who never haggle over price. It includes how to reduce stress and increase profits imme-diately. In addition, I will be available as a mentor to support you all the way.

If you want to know more about how I can help you, just give me a call at:

1 800 723 199
.

Or access my internet site at:
www.tradesmanprofits.com

I also wanted to tell you about some of the companies with which I have worked and that have the highest integrity possible in the business world. If you have the opportu-nity to do business with these great compa-nies, do not hesitate, and in addition I highly recommend them!

There have been four companies that have really stood out as the best of the best in my experiences in business. When I told them I was writing a book to help other tradesmen, I also told them I wanted to rec-ognize and thank them for the outstanding loyalty and service they have provided me over the years.

I also asked them if they would like to offer something to my readers because I have no reservations in giving any of them my personal testimonial.

Phil McCarroll Toyota - Hornsby
www.mccarrolls.com.au/toyota

I have owned many different kinds of vehicles over the years. In my latest business, I ran a fleet of over 25 vehicles with 60 staff. In all the time I've had a fleet, there has only been one brand of vehicle that has never let me down since I started in business and that is Toyota.

I bought all of my Toyotas from Phil McCarroll Toyota in Hornsby. Incredibly, out of the 10 Toyotas I have owned over ten years not one of them has ever broken down or so much as had a flat tire.

As a special promotion for the readers of this book Phil has offered $1,000 off any Toyota purchased from him. There is a voucher for Phil MacCarroll Toyota at the end of this book which you can bring to Phil for the discount.

Actron Air
www.actronair.com.au

Air conditioning systems from Actron Air are by far the finest ducted air conditioning systems I have ever installed, and I can tell you, that is a few air conditioners! Their performance and high quality has made it possible for me to guarantee the temperature in people's homes. Out of over 7000 instal-lations Actron Air systems have consistently had the highest performance and the lowest breakdown of any air conditioning system I have ever installed. My business success is therefore due to a large extent to their excel-lent product! Thank you, Actron Air!

Advantage Air
www.advantageair.com.au

I have already mentioned Advantage Air and the amazing support they gener-ously gave me when I went bankrupt. Even though I owed them the most money of any of my suppliers, they were extraordinarily kind to me.

Advantage Air makes the best air condi-tioning components I have ever used, they have a very unique patented system that makes their ductwork one of the most aero-dynamic systems possible. So, if you are ever looking for an air conditioning system then I strongly recommend that you use an Actron Air conditioner with the Advantage Air com-ponents.

I want to formally thank everyone at Ad-vantage Air, especially the General Manager David Devoy who's unwavering encourage-ment and support at one of the most difficult times in my life, meant more to me than he will ever know.

IAN MARSH

Marsh Air Marketing

I especially want to thank the company called BBY International that bought my wife's company Marsh Air Marketing after we built it up into a business that was turning eight million dollars a year in just eight month's time. I selected them from four buyers because of the owner's integrity.

As you know, I hold personal honesty and integrity in business very highly and Simon Bailey has very similar philosophies to mine. He also provides guarantees in the industry far exceeding those offered by any other company. He guarantees the temperature in your home and he gives a 10 year warranty on any installation done by his company.

If you have the chance, you should definitely patronize this fine company for your air conditioning system needs.

"Announcing The Streetsmart Tradesman Of The Year Challenge"

I am launching one of the biggest challenges ever, to any tradesman willing to take it on!

Challenge starts
1st of October, 2007
Awarded 30th of November 2008

2007 TOYOTA SR5
Diesel Four Wheel Drive
With Satellite Navigation.
Total Value: $52,000.00

As part of my new tradesmen's systems opportunity, I want to give you an additional incentive and encourage you to make your business the best it can be!

To do this, I am issuing a challenge. Starting October 1, 2007, I am giving every tradesman that uses my system the opportunity to compete with all the other participating tradesmen for a 2007 Toyota SR5 truck. The truck will be awarded to the tradesmen that is the best customer service tradesman company in Australia at the end of the year. Any size business is eligible, it is based totally on the difference you make in your company during the challenge.

I am excited to see the improvement I know everyone can make, and see just how high you can build your business!

In addition, $100 from every challenger will be donated to The Starlight Children's Foundation Australia.

Free 30 Minute Consultation With Ian!* A $250 Value!

If you are truly interested in either starting a new tradesman's business or improving your existing business, and you have bought this book, this offer is for you! I want to help tradesmen have a great income and a great lifestyle with a tradesman's business. Because of this, I am willing to dedicate a half hour of my time to you, a $250 value for free!

To redeem this offer, just clip the bar code off the back cover of this book, and the Free Value Sticker off the front cover and send them both along with your name, address, e-mail and phone number to:

Ian Marsh
30 Minute Consultation Offer
P.O Box 583
Windsor
NSW 2756

I will contact you and set up a consultation time where we can discuss your business, or you can just ask me questions. There are no strings attached, and your personal information will be kept strictly confidential. I look forward to hearing from you!
- Ian Marsh

*Offer expires October 10, 2008 and is void where taxed, regulated or prohibited. This offer may be cancelled without notice.

IAN MARSH

McCARROLL'S

THE BLOKES FROM THE BUSH

THIS VOUCHER IS WORTH

$1000

OFF ANY TOYOTA AT

Phil McCarroll Toyota
42-54 Pacific Highway, Waitara NSW 2077

Expires October 10th 2008

www.ingramcontent.com/pod-product-compliance
Lightning Source LLC
Chambersburg PA
CBHW021335090426
42742CB00008B/617